D0907057

OCT 1 1 2012

THE SPONSORSHIP HANDBOOK

THE SPONSORSHIP HANDBOOK

ESSENTIAL TOOLS, TIPS AND

TECHNIQUES FOR SPONSORS AND

SPONSORSHIP SEEKERS

PIPPA COLLETT AND WILLIAM FENTON

JOSSEY-BASS
A Wiley Imprint
www.josseybass.com

This edition first published in 2011

Copyright © 2011 Pippa Collett and William Fenton

Under the Jossey-Bass imprint, Jossey-Bass, 989 Market Street, San Francisco CA 94103-1741, USA

www.jossey-bass.com

Registered office

John Wiley & Sons Ltd, The Atrium, Southern Gate, Chichester, West Sussex, PO19 8SQ, United Kingdom

For details of our global editorial offices, for customer services and for information about how to apply for permission to reuse the copyright material in this book please see our website at www.wiley.com

The right of the authors to be identified as the authors of this work has been asserted in accordance with the Copyright, Designs and Patents Act 1988.

All rights reserved. No part of this publication may be reproduced, stored in a retrieval system, or transmitted, in any form or by any means, electronic, mechanical, photocopying, recording or otherwise, except as permitted by the UK Copyright, Designs and Patents Act 1988, without the prior permission of the publisher.

Wiley also publishes its books in a variety of electronic formats. Some content that appears in print may not be available in electronic books.

Designations used by companies to distinguish their products are often claimed as trademarks. All brand names and product names used in this book are trade names, service marks, trademarks or registered trademarks of their respective owners. The publisher is not associated with any product or vendor mentioned in this book. This publication is designed to provide accurate and authoritative information in regard to the subject matter covered. It is sold on the understanding that the publisher is not engaged in rendering professional services. If professional advice or other expert assistance is required, the services of a competent professional should be sought.

Library of Congress Cataloging-in-Publication Data

Fenton, William (William Seaborne), 1957-

  The Sponsorship Handbook : Essential Tools, Tips and Techniques for Sponsors and Sponsorship Seekers / William Fenton and Pippa Collett.

       p. cm

  Includes bibliographical references and index.

  ISBN 978-0-470-97984-6

  1. Corporate sponsorship.   I. Collett, Pippa.   II. Title.

  HD59.35.F46 2011

  659.2–dc22

                                                        2010050392

A catalogue record for this book is available from the British Library.

ISBN 978-0-470-97984-6 (hardback), ISBN 978-0-470-98002-6 (ebk),
ISBN 978-0-470-98000-2 (ebk), ISBN 978-0-470-98001-9 (ebk)

Typeset in 10/14.5pt FF Scala by Toppan Best-set Premedia Limited

Printed in Great Britain by TJ International Ltd, Padstow, Cornwall, UK

This book is dedicated to the pioneers of modern sponsorship, the colleagues and companies that have enabled us to develop our sponsorship competence and the patience and good humour of our families.

CONTENTS

FOREWORD

The European Sponsorship Association's mission is to improve the standards of professionalism in sponsorship practice and The Sponsorship Handbook makes a significant contribution to achieving this objective.

It is a practical guide to the key components of sponsorship with tools and checklists to prompt thinking and action. The many case studies drawn from sources all around the world help to illustrate key points and provide inspiration. The authors are sponsorship professionals with extensive, quality experience working both within and for leading sponsors and rights-holders.

As the sponsorship industry grows and new organizations enter the market. The Sponsorship Handbook will be a vital resource in educating new sponsors, rights-holders and other interested parties in sponsorship best practice.

Karen Earl
Chairman
European Sponsorship Association

PREFACE

As a relatively young marketing discipline, sponsorship lacks the body of knowledge required to ensure best practice and the implementation of policies and processes that result in satisfactory outcomes. As full time practitioners and part time lecturers, with more than 40 years sponsorship experience between us, we wanted to capture what we have learned, often through trial and error, to help newcomers to this exciting industry learn more quickly and less painfully than we did!

This book aims to create a baseline understanding of sponsorship by introducing anyone interested in developing their sponsorship competence to the principles and processes that will enable them to deliver robust results.

For further resources and information on sponsorship visit http://www.sponsorshipstore.com.

For updates on news, ideas and trends in sponsorship follow us on Twitter @Sponsorshiptips.

ABOUT THE AUTHORS

Pippa Collett

Pippa Collett is a leading sponsorship practitioner with an extensive client-side career with Shell, American Express and Rank Organization. Her global sponsorship experience includes Ferrari in Formula One motor racing and the Athens Olympics as well as arts and entertainment projects such as The Olivier Awards and Disneyland Paris. She joined Sponsorship Consulting as Managing Director in 2006 to work with blue-chip clients such as Siemens, Standard Chartered Bank and Cisco.

Achieving measurable returns on sponsorship investments is a particular interest, and her work in this area was recognized with a Hollis Award for Best Use of Research in Sponsorship in 2005. As Vice-Chair of The European Sponsorship Association, Pippa has led on key aspects of the developing sponsorship agenda, including authorship of ESA's Sponsorship Assessment & Evaluation Guidelines and introducing the concept of Continuing Professional Development. More recently she has developed ESA's Sponsorship Agency Selection Process and is currently focusing on developing the structure for the provision of qualifications within the sponsorship industry across Europe.

An occasional lecturer at the Institute of Direct Marketing and the Incorporated Society of British Advertisers, Pippa is a regular speaker at sponsorship conferences in the US, UK, Europe and the Middle East. Her work has been published in the *Journal of Sponsorship*, *The International Journal of Sports Marketing & Sponsorship*, and *Argent*, the journal of the Financial Services Forum. Her opinion on sponsorship issues is widely sought by the media, including the BBC, CNBC, *The Times* and the *Wall Street Journal* as well as the marketing trade press.

A Cranfield MBA, Founder Chartered Marketer, Fellow of the RSA and member of the Marketing Society, Pippa lives in London with her husband and two children and is a keen carriage driver.

William Fenton

William Fenton is a Director of Sponsorship Consulting in London and Brussels, looking after clients as diverse as The British Library, The Dubai International Film Festival, Epson, FedEx, The Olympic Business Club and The European Space Agency. His status as a sponsorship expert has been built through 19 years in sponsorship, working with IFM Sports Marketing Surveys and Sponsorship Research International/ISL on major sports events including the Olympics, FIFA World Cup and Formula One racing.

William is Editor of *The World Sponsorship Monitor* produced by IFM Sports Marketing Surveys and has been published in *The International Journal of Sports Marketing & Sponsorship, The Journal of Sponsorship* and *SportBusiness International,* as well as making appearances on CNBC television's *Money and Sport* programme. He lectures at the Hogeschool-Universiteit and VUB University in Brussels, holds the Market Research Society Advanced Certificate in Market and Social Research Practice and is a founder member of the European Sponsorship Association's Continuing Professional Development Accreditation programme.

Based in Brussels, married with three children and a keen rower since his time at Durham University, his earliest practical experience of securing and managing sponsorship goes back to the £2.5 million 1986 *In The Footsteps of Scott* Expedition. Reputed as the "last great 20th-century expedition", three men were the first to successfully walk the 900 miles to the South Pole without support. Sponsors of Captain Scott's original 1912 expedition returned 74 years later and a Jonathan Cape book and a contract with ITN News helped to secure the huge logistical budget. This included an aircraft and a ship, *The Southern Quest,* which sank spectacularly in Antarctic ice on the return journey without loss of life, and with William on board. The images were seen by viewers across the world.

ACKNOWLEDGEMENTS

Christine Hutton; Suzanne Millington; Graeme Davis (Sponsorship Consulting); David Lapish (O2); Michael Brockbank (Unilever); Jos Cleare (Accenture); Darren Marshall (Evolution); David Sleigh (Footbalance); Caroline Booth (Telecom New Zealand); Amy Lyddall Fell (Nelsons); Farina Jabbari (Nelsons); Guido Becchis (Youthstream); Annemie Vander Vorst (FedEx); Gwendolyn Da Silva (Morgan Stanley); Daragh Persee (Vodafone); Pia DeVitre (Deloitte); Jacob Vanluchene (Red Bull); Anne Keogh (Siemens); Claire Jarvis (Siemens); Leilani Yan (AirAdvertainment); Alastair Marks (McDonald's); Gareth Roberts (Carlsberg); Shaun Whatling (Redmandarin); Lesa Ukman (IEG); Tony Ponturo (Ponturo Management Group); Fiona Seymour (Department of Transport); Nigel Geach (IFM Sports Marketing Surveys); Sandra Greer (IFM Sports Marketing Surveys); Jeff Eccleston (Sponsorship Research International – SRi); Ardi Kolah (Guru in a Bottle); Karen Earl (European Sponsorship Association); Jos Verschueren (Vrije Universiteit, Brussel Faculty of Physical Education and Physiotherapy Department of Sports Policy and Management); Jaclyn Neal (Beiersdorf UK Ltd); Nicola Seery (Beiersdorf UK Ltd); Zoe Stainsby (Cake); Simon Fry (FedEx); Faisal Dail (Saudi Post); Luis Vicente (Manchester City Football Club); Serena Hedley-Dent (Farrer & Co) and Ben Treadaway & Mark Cornish (Sponsorium).
Formula One is a trademark of Formula One Licensing B.V.

Disclaimer

Whilst every attempt has been made to credit third parties (where applicable) and all care has been taken to represent information accurately and in good faith, the authors shall not be responsible for any errors or omissions, factual or otherwise, and do not accept any liability arising out of any reliance placed on information contained within this publication. The authors would, however, welcome any correction to credits or of materials contained within this publication for future editions.

HOW TO USE THIS BOOK

The sections for sponsors and sponsorship seekers both inform each other as the key to good sponsorship is understanding the needs and different perspectives of both parties. Icons are used to guide the reader and make it easier to extract information quickly.

     Overview

     Case Study

     Key Action

     Key Questions

     Key Learning Points

CHAPTER 1

INTRODUCTION TO SPONSORSHIP

Overview

Sponsorship, correctly conceived and creatively executed, has unparalleled power to build brands, engage stakeholders and present profitable commercial opportunities.

This chapter introduces the basic building blocks required to understand sponsorship and the environment in which it operates, including:

- What sponsorship is, and is not, in the context of modern sponsorship practice.
- The size of the industry, and why it continues to see growth at a time when advertising spend is slowing.
- The key players and the range of sponsorship opportunities, target audiences and possible sponsorship objectives that should be taken into consideration.
- Tangible and intangible sponsorship assets and how some of these might be valued.
- The process of sponsorship from both a sponsor's and a rights-holder's perspective.
- A discussion about when to use internal headcount versus external support to deliver on sponsorship objectives.

Sponsorship: what is it?

This is the subject of much current debate especially with take up of social media which we discuss in Chapter 10. At best, sponsorship is an associative marketing tool that creates mutual brand and business value for both the sponsor and the sponsored activity. At worst, it is an excuse for the Chairman to indulge his wife's interests at the shareholders' expense. The most widely accepted definition currently is that of the International Chamber of Commerce:

> "Any commercial agreement by which a sponsor, for the mutual benefit of the sponsor and sponsored party, contractually provides financing or other support in order to establish an association between the sponsor's image, brands or products and a sponsorship property in return for rights to promote this association and/or for the granting of certain agreed direct or indirect benefits."

The key words in this rather long statement are:

- *Commercial:* Modern sponsorship of the sort undertaken by businesses large and small is targeted at delivering some sort of commercial outcome for business owners, whether the company is publicly or privately owned. The benefits may be accrued in terms of additional revenues or cost savings in the profit and loss account, or as an increase in the value of brand equity on the balance sheet. While an individual undertaking a challenge to raise money for good causes – such as running a marathon or learning a new skill – is a laudable activity, it is outside the scope of this definition, and therefore this book.
- *Mutual:* There is progressive acceptance that the benefits of a sponsorship relationship should represent a win–win partnership for both the sponsor's organization and that of the sponsored activity.
- *Contract:* This may be written out in detail or be based on an oral agreement, but the fundamentals of contract law, as applied in the appropriate judicial system, will apply to the relationship. The rights-holder is offering

for sale the right of association and possibly other benefits, which are accepted by the sponsor and confirmed by the provision of some form of consideration, which may be cash or defined value in kind. An informal agreement of mutual association with no consideration does not constitute sponsorship under the ICC definition.

This definition therefore excludes many activities that historically might have been given the name of sponsorship, such as philanthropy, donations or patronage. However, one of the reasons the definition of sponsorship is currently causing such controversy is the development of other associative marketing activities that, from the average consumer's standpoint, look and feel like some sort of sponsorship (see Figure 1.1). These include:

- *Cause-related marketing* – Red, the global AIDS-related fundraising initiative, is a good example where a variety of brands have come together to raise money to fight AIDS while benefiting from enhanced brand equity.
- *Product placement* – Whether it is BMW in the Bond movies or Coca-Cola being prominently consumed by X Factor USA judges, consumers are progressively aware that brands are capitalizing on collective aspirations to market their products.
- *Advertiser-funded programming* – Gillette's World of Sport is the classic example of the genre, associating shaving products with performance.

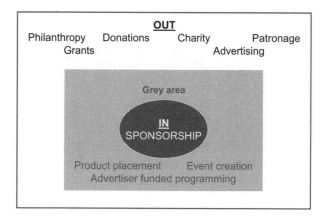

Figure 1.1 Pictorial representation of the definition of sponsorship

- *Event creation* – The Red Bull Air Race or Nike 10k Runs look like sponsored events but are both in fact owned by the relevant brand, representing a desire by them to have more control of the activity than would normally be available in a true sponsorship relationship.

This book will largely limit itself to the discussion of those principles and processes that relate to the core sponsorship definition, but it should be understood that many of those issues will also be applicable to other activities within the associative marketing spectrum.

Industry development

Sponsorship has experienced unprecedented growth over the last decade, with the level of investment in purchasing sponsorship rights of association almost doubling (see Figure 1.2).

This compares favourably with the growth in spend on advertising over the same period. Of particular note is the continued growth in sponsorship

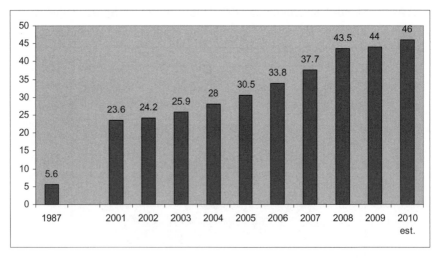

Figure 1.2 Global sponsorship rights spend USD billions, 1987–2010
(Reproduced with permission of IEG)

during the 2008–9 recession, albeit at a slower rate than previous years, at a time when advertising spend contracted by around 5%. The increased investment in sponsorship is underpinned by three core trends: economic development, social evolution, and the technological revolution.

- Economic development is currently focusing attention on sponsorship as a marketing tool because of the aspirations that greater economic freedom brings to individuals. In agrarian society wealth is highly concentrated with the majority existing at or below subsistence level with nothing to spare for discretionary activity. Economic development creates both the time and the cash for individuals to spend on discretionary items, usually initially allocated to physical comfort. As prosperity becomes the norm, so more money is available to allocate, first, to burden-reducing services, and then to leisure pursuits. Fully mature markets have now moved into an experience economy where people are looking for self-actualizing experiences. This is a need to which brands are responding, whether it is the "terrific experience" of dining at Pizza Hut, shopping at Apple or applying a grooming product. The challenge for many brands is to make these experiences real for customers. Sponsorship facilitates the bringing alive of brand experiences.
- Social evolution is the second trend driving growth in the sponsorship industry. Historically people identified themselves by the feudal lord they served. More recently, identity was linked to the company that provided your employment. Similarly, women started to gain their own identity, no longer recognized as merely their father's daughter or husband's wife. The outcomes of these societal changes are that people are looking for new badges of allegiance. These may be found in politics, sport, religion or other pursuits which bind groups together in real or virtual communities at the consumer level.

  This social evolution has also impacted how corporations see their role in society. The introduction of triple bottom line accounting has meant that companies can no longer focus merely on economic success in terms of profit and dividends. Now they also have to consider their social and environmental impact. This has led companies to invest at grass roots levels in education, health, sport and culture, aiming not only to make a contribution at the local community level but also to have a global impact.

Figure 1.3 Communication channel development, 1958–2011

■ However, the technological revolution represents the most important trend for sponsorship. The shift from a limited number of one-way channels to a plethora of two-way interactions has dramatically changed our expectations as consumers (see Figure 1.3).

There has been a fundamental shift from the interruption advertising and brand monologue of the 20th century to a multi-channel approach requiring brands to apply a multi-niche strategy. Consumers can now tap into multiple sources of information and no longer have to take a brand advertisement on trust. People very much want to have a dialogue with brands and, while some brands are finding this quite uncomfortable, winners in the long term will be those that learn to adapt to an interactive audience. Targeting based on socio-demographic groups is becoming ineffective because new communities incorporate a wide range of different types. So, businesses are looking much more at how they target communities of people with similar habits and behaviours rather than merely their socio-demographic grouping.

The challenge of the new communications reality is that it has had a huge impact on the consumer in terms of their ability to identify and absorb information. As Seth Goodin identifies in his book *Permission Marketing*, "the days of high demand and limited supply are over ... it's a new game now. A game where the limited supply is attention." *Advertising* is excellent for generating awareness, *public relations* informs and influences, and *sales promotion* stimulates trial, but all compete with each other to cut through the marketing clutter.

Brands have found that the best way to get our attention is to identify the passions of new communities and align with them through *sponsorship*.

The basic building blocks of sponsorship

Essential to successful sponsorship is an understanding of the key components that make up the industry. It is critical that all parties are aware of the other constituents and the role these play in terms of their collective ability to deliver on the rights assigned (see Figure 1.4).

The concept of a property and a sponsor may be considered as rather simplistic when placed within the environment of the sponsorship industry as a whole. The first challenge is to define exactly who is the rights-holder, that is, the organization that has the authority to sell the rights of association to a sponsor. Most often the rights-holder is the property's management, such as the Guggenheim Museum selling sponsorship for an art exhibition. However, there are occasions, and particularly in broadcast sponsorship, where the rights-holder is not directly overseeing the property itself, and this is being undertaken by some intermediary.

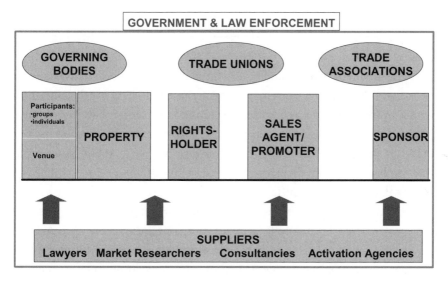

Figure 1.4 The key components of the sponsorship industry

Case Study: The Olympic and Paralympic Games

Key learning points:

- Be absolutely clear which organization is able to sell you which rights.
- You may need to contract with a number of organizations to achieve all the rights required to implement and leverage a sponsorship successfully.

A good example of this is the relationship between the International Olympic Committee (IOC) and the National Olympic Committee (NOC). The IOC ultimately controls all the rights to Olympic Marks, logos and symbols and sells them directly to their global sponsors. However, the IOC also delegates the opportunity to sell rights of association to the Olympics – although not the Marks, logos and symbols – to all the NOCs within their national boundaries. It would be most unfortunate if a brand negotiated an agreement with an NOC for rights of association with the Olympics with the assumption that this gave the brand the right to use the Olympic rings logo, or to promote an association with the Olympics globally.

More frequent in sport and entertainment than in culture is the use of a sales agent or promoter. They may have purchased the right to sell association with a property as a sponsorship opportunity but may not have the right to include database access, for example. If database access were important to a brand as part of a potential sponsorship relationship it would be essential that the brand identify the party that could grant database access rights and ensure that these were contractually agreed.

One group that people often forget when thinking about a property are the "performers". For example, if sponsoring a performance at La Scala was under consideration, it is most likely that negotiations would occur direct with the Opera House's management. However, if the soloists were expected to attend a post-performance party and socialize, further agreements might need to be negotiated with the performers or via their agents. Equally, if a brand wanted to conduct spectator activation as part of sponsoring Six Nations Rugby, there might be a need to have separate agreements with the venues such as Twickenham, Murrayfield or Stade de France as well as purchasing rights of association with the Six Nations from the International Rugby Board.

Underpinning the core sponsorship relationship, there may also be a wide variety of suppliers, including lawyers to write tailored contracts, market researchers, consultancies or activation agencies. Also influencing the relationship may be the governing bodies of sport or trade unions such as Equity for the performing arts world, or trade associations and, of course, sponsorships must conform to government legislation and law enforcement.

The concept of a sponsor, that is, a corporation that invests cash or in kind in return for the right to associate its brand with a sponsored "property", is largely understood.

The sponsored property may be an event or activity that is individual or infrastructural in nature. Figure 1.5 gives a number of examples of possible sponsorship opportunities.

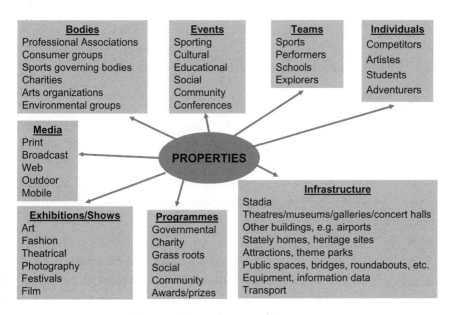

Figure 1.5 Types of sponsorship property

Figure 1.6 Potential target audiences for sponsorships

Sports are the most widely recognized sponsorship vehicles, and gain the lion's share of sponsorship investment, followed by broadcast and culture. However, there are a large number of potential sponsorship opportunities and these should all be taken into consideration when identifying the "best fit" for a particular sponsor's needs.

Outside the sponsorship industry itself are the people that the sponsorship is aimed at impacting in some way – specifically, the target audience(s) (see Figure 1.6). The most frequent target audience for sponsorship is consumers, with the aim of changing attitudes and behaviours towards the sponsoring brand or corporation, thus creating value in the profit and loss (P&L) account or balance sheet. A number of organizations also use sponsorship to support change internally, focusing on how they can educate and engage their employees.

However, there are many other potential target audiences against which sponsorship can be deployed successfully. Within the value chain, sponsorships may be aimed at changing behaviours among suppliers, wholesalers or retailers to positively impact value delivered. Alternatively, sponsorships may have analysts or key Government departments as their primary focus. Equally, sponsorship could be targeted at influencing the media and how they report on the corporation.

There are many excellent examples of sponsorships aimed at improving relationships with NGOs or local communities. For example, a big manufacturing plant might invest in sponsorships that engage the local community, demonstrating a desire to compensate in some relevant way for the noise or light pollution the plant creates.

The essential key to successful sponsorship lies ultimately in having clearly defined sponsorship objectives. In its Sponsorship Assessment and Evaluation Guidelines, the European Sponsorship Association (ESA) distinguished three different groups of sponsorship objectives (see Figure 1.7).

The most widely recognized group of objectives is focused around brand building, from creating brand awareness through to promoting brand advocacy.

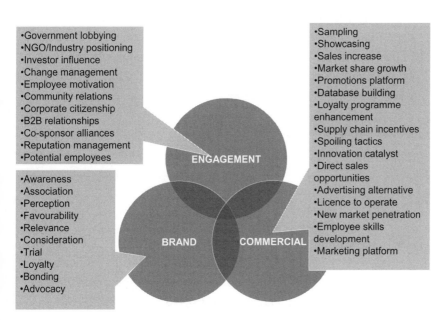

Figure 1.7 Possible sponsorship objectives
(Source: European Sponsorship Association, reproduced with permission)

Case Study: Vodafone

 Key learning points:

- Exposure measurement is valid if one of your sponsorship objectives is to obtain visibility for a young brand.
- In this case, the Ferrari sponsorship's ability to provide global exposure was deemed to be more cost effective and more engaging than buying commercial airtime.

Vodafone's entry into Formula One racing as a sponsor of the Scuderia Ferrari team followed a period of acquisitions for the mobile communications company through which it had expanded its network to multiple markets around the world. While the sponsorship also had differentiation, engagement and revenue objectives, generating broad awareness for the brand on a global scale at a time when the brand was expanding into new markets was a key deliverable. Formula One, with a minimum 2 hours of television coverage every fortnight for 8 months of the year, presented a cost-effective platform through which to reach 350 million viewers globally – a high percentage of which represented a key target audience for Vodafone.

(Reproduced with permission of Vodafone)

 Case Study: O2

 Key learning points:

- While a sponsorship may provide a lot of brand exposure, there may be more important underlying objectives to be achieved.

continued on next page ...

- When assessing sponsorship investments, where relevant consider whether it will be possible to scale up as a sponsor's needs change.

At the other end of the brand-building scale, European mobile telecoms brand O2 took title rights to the O2 sport and entertainment facility in Greenwich, London and other entertainment venues across the UK. The focus here is on priority booking for O2 customers to drive brand loyalty and advocacy, and the concept has been so successful that O2 has replicated it in Ireland, Germany and the Czech Republic.

(Reproduced with permission of O2)

For some brands, sponsorship is much more about a direct line of sight to commercial benefits. ESA also identified a long, but not exhaustive, list of possible commercial objectives for sponsorship (see Figure 1.7).

 Case Study: Nivea For Men®

 Key learning point:

- There is nothing wrong with being highly commercial in your sponsorship objectives, as long as leveraging activities are aligned with fans' needs and enhancing their experience.

An excellent example of a product-sampling oriented sponsorship is that of Nivea For Men®, which became the official grooming partner of Powerleague Five-a-side football centres. This included the branding rights and provision of samples in all 42 Powerleague centres. As well as sampling activity, there were a series of targeted competitions and promotions giving away free play hours and team match places at

continued on next page ...

Powerleague centres throughout the UK, culminating with a five-a-side football tournament in the summer.

(*Reproduced with permission of Beiersdorf UK Ltd*)

 Case Study: Oil companies and Formula One

 Key learning points:

- Commercial objectives for sponsorship may not directly contribute to the bottom line, but there should be a line of sight between the investment and potential returns.
- Sponsorships should still make intuitive sense to the average consumer when they are translated from the sponsorship environment to retail.

Another example, this time of using sponsorship as a catalyst for innovation, is the relationship between oil companies and Formula One motor racing. To speed up the pace of everyday road fuel development, the oil majors task their scientists to provide lighter, more efficient fuels that allow race cars to travel faster and cover greater distances on the race track. Often the scientists are present in the Paddock at the heart of the action and share the pain of defeat and pleasure of winning with the team they support. The drive to find new fuel and lubricants solutions to deliver even better racing results speeds up the development cycle. Relevant innovations can then be translated into the products available for everyday drivers at a service station.

Much of the sponsorship by international corporations in developing countries is about securing a license to operate. Investing in the sporting, cultural or educational development of a country is recognized as one way of thanking these communities for allowing the corporation to benefit from local resources, whether these are mining raw materials or more cost-effective labour solutions.

The third group of objectives as defined by ESA are those where the primary purpose is engagement with particular audiences and includes everything from government lobbying to employee motivation. Sponsorships could be structured around managing reputation in the marketplace or positioning the brand as a good employer to attract the best talent from among young graduates or school leavers. This group also incorporates developing business-to-business relationships via sponsorship-linked hospitality and educational experiences.

 Case Study: Siemens

 Key learning points:

- Employees are often an afterthought where sponsorship is concerned, but if your staff are not able to articulate your sponsorship rationale, how will they communicate it effectively to customers?
- Media exposure may help build brand awareness but it only delivers broad messages to a target audience. Targeted PR activity ensures your key messages are communicated through credible editorial.

Siemens plc, part of the global engineering group, successfully deployed its sponsorship of the GB rowing team both to engage employees via an indoor rowing competition while also leveraging the platform to nurture relationships with opinion-formers via carefully targeted PR activities.

(Reproduced with permission of Siemens plc)

The only problem with such a large number of possible objectives is that organizations often expect sponsorship to achieve many different goals. This results in fragmenting focus on the project and stretching budget too thinly across a wide range of activation programmes, thereby weakening the possibility of real demonstrable success. Two to three clearly defined objectives is probably the optimal number, with five as an absolute maximum.

Sponsorship assets

Sponsorship assets translate into the actual benefits a sponsor purchases through its sponsorship contract. Sponsorship assets can be divided into those that have a value that is *tangible,* that is, where the value can be defined in monetary terms, or *intangible,* where the value is non-financial. Some examples of both types of assets can be found in Table 1.1.

Tangible assets

Media exposure, or rather the value of the media exposure gained by a brand as a result of a sponsorship, is the most widely accepted asset sold by rights-holders, followed by tickets and hospitality opportunities. Media value is derived from calculating the amount of time the brand's logo is displayed on screen (or via posters and other media) and calculating the equivalent cost to

Table 1.1 Examples of tangible and intangible sponsorship assets

Tangible Assets Monetary value can be calculated	Intangible Assets Value is non-financial
Media exposure	Transferable brand attributes
Tickets/hospitality	Property prestige
Brand advertising opportunities	Quality of activity delivery
Database access	Convenience of location
Specialist knowledge/expertise	Credibility of brand endorsement
Meeting facilities	Degree of audience loyalty
Brand ambassadors	Category exclusivity
Sampling	Strength of shared goals
Technology	Networking opportunities
Administrative resources	Facilitated introductions
Content provision	Exclusivity of access
Marketing activity	Uncluttered environment

purchase the same air time as advertising. Tickets will have a face value and, although a sponsor's specific package may not be available on the open market, it is usually possible to find proxies that reflect the value of the elements offered.

The cost of purchasing an equivalent list from a list broker is a sound method for calculating the value of database access. Access to specialist knowledge and expertise can be valued by how much a sponsor would have to pay to buy that expertise itself in terms of a specialist employee. The provision of meeting facilities can be compared against the cost to rent the same sort of meeting room in a hotel or conference centre. Brand ambassadors can be judged against hiring an equivalent celebrity via a speaker bureau. The cost of setting up and staffing a booth in a high traffic location like a train station can be compared to the benefit of being able to provide sampling via a sponsorship relationship. Access to technology usually has an open market value, similarly administrative resources.

Access to content has become very important in many sponsorships, not least in the mobile phone and service provider markets as they seek to differentiate each brand. This content can either be "broadcast equivalent" or "exclusive access", but both can be valued either by the cost to purchase the content from a broadcaster or how much it would cost to organize a production company to go out and film the equivalent content. Finally, access to a rights-holder's marketing for the property can be calculated by the company considering the costs of carrying out a similar marketing programme.

Intangible assets

Intangible assets, in comparison, are often more difficult to assess in terms of value added. The value ascribed will vary widely depending on the relevance of any intangible asset to a particular sponsor and its bespoke sponsorship objectives.

Purchasing the right of association is the essence of any sponsorship relationship. It therefore follows that the most significant intangible asset sold by a rights-holder is the impact the sponsorship has on the sponsor's brand by virtue of transferable brand attributes from the sponsored property. The value of this benefit can fluctuate from minimal, where a sponsorship is

largely targeted at achieving commercial objectives, to being the most significant benefit in the sponsorship package. The best illustration of this is sponsorship of the Olympic Games where corporations pay multi-millions for the
rights of association and the ability to use Olympic Marks, logos and symbols.
Virtually everything else, including tickets and hospitality, has to be purchased in addition.

If a sponsorship is targeted at business-to-business engagement, the convenience of the property's location, its prestige and the quality with which it
is delivered – and therefore its ability to attract the target audience to attend
the hospitality – may be more important than marketing the rights of
association.

 Case Study: Morgan Stanley

 Key learning points:

- Cultural sponsorships, and visual arts in particular, lend themselves
  to delivering on a business-to-business orientated sponsorship
  agenda.
- The ability to view iconic art works at leisure without competing with
  the general public is a compelling proposition for busy executives.

A good example of this was Morgan Stanley's sponsorship of The First
Emperor: China's Terracotta Army at the British Museum which ran
from September 2007 to April 2008. The sponsorship gave Morgan
Stanley the opportunity to align their brand with their business interests
in China, while also providing a culturally innovative platform for
engaging with clients. Private views of the exhibition allowed clients the
privileged opportunity to view the terracotta warriors without the crowds
– providing a unique way for Morgan Stanley to deepen existing client
relationships as well as help to build new ones.

(Reproduced with permission of Morgan Stanley)

For some brands, especially those with a limited number of major competitors, it is really important to have exclusivity in their category in a sponsorship. For other brands it is actually the complete opposite: what they want is to be seen to be part of a peer group that helps to make them look bigger, stronger and more impressive than their accounts might justify.

It is also important that sponsors and rights-holders understand that their frames of reference may be completely different. This is illustrated in Table 1.2 where four different elements are compared. However, it is important to understand that there may be other issues on which rights-holders and corporations have a different perspective, and both need to be aware of this possibility in order to correctly interpret aspects of their relationship.

Sponsors are largely PLCs and are therefore driven by the shareholder imperative, which is to increase shareholder value not only in terms of the equity and share price, but also in terms of dividends paid. Accounting elements are the P&L account and the balance sheet, measuring value in terms of profit and equity, and leadership will be drawn from a cross-section of people with finely honed business skills and experience.

The sports rights-holder's perspective, as illustrated in Table 1.2, is often quite different. The business model is focused more on sporting success, with winning being the main performance measure. Most sports properties are not PLCs, cash flow is viewed as more important than profit and they are often led by sports enthusiasts. Of course, this can also be translated into culture, education or other sponsorship property categories. The desire for

Table 1.2 Different perspectives between sponsors and rights-holders

	Sponsor	Rights–holder
Business model	Shareholder imperative	"For the good of the game"
Accounting elements	P&L account	Cash flow
	Balance sheet	White knight
Performance measures	Share price	Winning
	Dividend	A full house
Human resources	Business Managers	Sports enthusiasts

curatorial integrity in cultural rights-holders can be as strong as the will to win among their sporting equivalents. Equally, most educationalists, while passionate about their work, have very little experience of the sharp end of the business world. The importance of understanding the different frames of reference between a sponsor and a rights-holder cannot be underestimated.

The process of sponsorship

In many ways the process of sponsorship is no different from any other process. It starts with developing the right strategy, good planning and efficient execution, and is brought together with a thorough evaluation. However, in sponsorship the application of this process varies somewhat when viewed through the different lenses of sponsor and rights-holder. Each section of the planning process will be discussed in detail in other chapters, so here only a brief overview is given to highlight the differences between the two perspectives.

Let us look initially at the sponsorship process from a sponsor's perspective (see Figure 1.8).

■ Developing or reviewing sponsorship strategy for sponsors is often the result of a change in business priorities or marketing direction, as it is imperative that sponsorship strategy is derived from these elements and contributes to business and marketing success. Putting a proper sponsorship policy in place and developing decision frameworks and selection

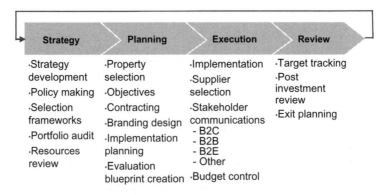

Figure 1.8 The process of sponsorship – for sponsors

criteria to guide future sponsorship investment decisions all flow from a robust sponsorship strategy. It also allows any current sponsorships to be reviewed to ensure that they remain fit for purpose. If not, the strategy will provide guidance on how best to exit gracefully. Most importantly, clarifying what resources will be available, both in terms of money and personnel, will be critical to driving the new strategy forward successfully.

- From a planning perspective, thinking will be centered around identifying and selecting the right properties, establishing clear objectives for each property and satisfactorily concluding the contracting phase. Once a robust agreement is in place, effort will focus on constructing and gaining internal support for a sponsorship activation programme, developing the branding model for promoting rights of association and creating the blueprint for evaluation.

- In many respects the first two phases of the sponsorship process are somewhat internal, while execution is where the majority of an organization's energy and resources are expended. Success will be judged on how well the programme plan is implemented, bringing the sponsorship to life and engaging stakeholders, whether consumers, business-to-business or employees. Appropriate suppliers may need to be found to supplement internal resources or bring specialist experience and expertise into play and, of course, the budget will need close attention.

- Finally, there is the evaluation phase. In fact, successful evaluation requires having milestones in place and tracking sponsorship performance throughout the execution phase. Formal performance discussions and post investment reviews are essential to identifying, capturing and implementing new ideas to improve outcomes in the future. Sponsorships that fail their performance hurdles will need careful exit planning.

Looking at it from the perspective of rights-holders, the process is the same but the emphasis is slightly different (see Figure 1.9).

- Sponsorship strategy for rights-holders focuses on what is the most appropriate approach to sponsorship and how best to position the property to attract sponsorship investment. Identifying sponsorship assets and understanding their potential value is critical, but rights-holders also have to allocate the appropriate resources if they wish to optimize sponsorship

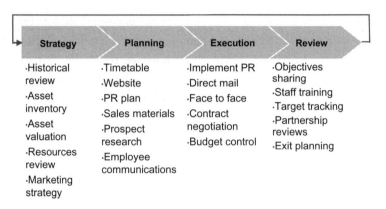

Figure 1.9 The process of sponsorship – for rights-holders

value creation. Finally, the best marketing strategy for the rights must be agreed.

■ Moving forward into planning, rights-holders must have a clear timetable about (a) how they are going to sell their rights and implement partnerships, (b) what they need to do with their website and PR plan to attract sponsor interest, and (c) how they are going to develop their sales materials. Thorough prospect research is essential to identify those organizations that are the hottest prospects to target. Ensuring that employees understand the approach and how they can potentially help to bring new partners on board is crucial to sponsorship-seeking success.

■ The execution phase comes in two parts. The first is the sales effort to attract sponsors, undertaking face-to-face meetings and finalizing contract negotiations. Perhaps more important is actually implementing those partnerships. Too many rights-holders focus their effort on securing the sale then do themselves a disservice by failing to adequately service their sponsors. Understanding the objectives of both parties, and making the sponsor's activation happen within the budget, will be critical in retaining the sponsor for the long term.

■ The review phase for rights-holders should also focus on target tracking against sponsor's objectives. Many rights-holders overlook this, thinking it is an unnecessary cost, but it is very powerful to be able to prove to a sponsor how the property has delivered against their objectives when con-

ducting a re-signing discussion. This is even better if sponsorship fulfill-
ment reports have been provided on a regular basis. Rights-holders will also
need to do some exit planning. This may be both from the point of view of
what happens if the sponsor does not re-sign for a further term, or possibly
that the rights-holder has outgrown a particular sponsor and needs to have
the freedom to move on.

? The in-source/out-source debate

One of the biggest issues both brands and rights-holders face is whether to
allocate precious internal headcount to manage a sponsorship programme or
to seek external support to develop and/or implement sponsorship effectively.
There are strengths and weaknesses in both approaches, as highlighted in
Table 1.3.

The strength of the internal solution is that employees will tend to be
better aligned with corporate strategies because they are surrounded by
an organization that is hopefully working in a single direction. A manager
will have tight control of direct employees and, if they have been with the

Table 1.3 Strengths and weaknesses of resourcing options

	Internal Resources	External Resources
Strengths	• "On strategy" • Tight control • Internal networks	• Easier to get rid of • Overcomes credibility/ politics • Resourcing flexibility • Speed to market • Specialist experience
Weaknesses	• Time consuming • Headcount • Hidden costs: time, resources	• Culture clash • Staff turnover • Perceived high cost

organization for any length of time, these employees will have informal networks that will help them to get things done.

Of course, from a different perspective, managing people is time consuming, headcount is always an issue for large organizations and there are hidden costs in having people in terms of their time – how much time they actually spend working versus chatting at the water cooler – and the cost of their desk, lighting, heating, power and other benefits normally provided to regular employees. Most organizations work on 100% of salary as an overhead charge, which illustrates just how much those hidden expenses of having an employee might actually cost.

On the external side the strengths are that it is easier to get rid of external resources and they can overcome any sort of credibility or internal politics issues. They can be very flexible, so they can staff up to meet a particular event need and then rapidly scale back again and they can help you to get to market very quickly. If a sponsorship is signed late, external resources will help to optimize the outcomes of that sponsorship. And of course they have specialist experience that may not be available internally.

The issues around external resources are that they may well have a culture clash with the hiring organization as agency staff may be accustomed to working in a relatively more fast-moving environment. Inevitably agencies have higher staff turnover which may destabilize a combined internal/agency team and cause problems until an acceptable replacement is found. Finally, because agency costs are very transparent – they sit as a clear line in a marketing budget – they do have a perceived high cost compared to internal resources where a lot of costs are hidden.

So, when faced with this conundrum, the recommendation is to resource internally in the following scenarios:

- The sponsorship activity is part of the core customer value proposition. Adidas or Nike manage their sponsorship internally because the performance of their apparel or footwear in a sporting context is key to the customer value proposition being promoted to the broad consumer audience.

- The necessary skills are available and accessible in-house and are not fully deployed on other sponsorship activities.
- The activity is of critical value to the company. For example, in the context of professional services firms, business-to-business customer contact is very important. Therefore, many of these organizations have big event management departments to manage closely every aspect of each event, optimizing the outcomes for their organization. Equally, from a rights-holder point of view, if sponsorship forms a relatively minor part of the organization's funding, then external resources are fine. However, if generating revenue from sponsorship is key to actually making an event or activity happen, then investing in internal resources will be beneficial in the long run.
- The right resources are not available externally for one reason or another, in which case there is no choice, apart from not doing the activity at all, to finding internal resources.

Of course outsourcing does have its place and should be given due consideration before final decisions are made. The key reasons to seek third party assistance are:

- Accessing best practice where specialist skills are needed but they are not essential to the business's core competence and therefore not worth the time and energy required to hire internally.
- Improving the quality of service that can be provided, especially where external staff can specialize while internal personnel may be more generalist.
- Where speed to market is critical and there is not enough time to identify and grow internal resources effectively.
- To maintain cost discipline through transparency of costs, perhaps where clarity of return on total investment outcomes will impact budget allocations in future.
- To benefit from resourcing flexibility, especially where activities are seasonal and headcount may not be fully utilized some of the time.
- Minimization of human resources administration internally, as agencies will tend to be able to manage less expensively than large corporations and institutions.

- Overcoming those internal barriers where an external supplier delivers the perceived authority or the impartial advice that helps an organization to move forward on something to which they are, perhaps, emotionally too close.

 Key take-outs

- The sponsorship industry is strong and growing due to its ability to allow brands and corporations to engage with audiences in meaningful ways.
- The building blocks of successful sponsorship deployment are complex and need due consideration in developing and implementing a sponsorship strategy.
- Rights-holders and sponsors may have widely differing drivers and these need to be understood and taken into account when developing sponsorship relationships.
- The process of sponsorship is not very different for the two key parties, but the different emphases should not be overlooked.
- There are both pros and cons for building in-house competence versus potentially outsourcing to third-party specialists.

Summary

Sponsorship is a complex marketing tool and the work required to implement effective sponsorship programmes on behalf of an organization should not be underestimated. Nevertheless, it is currently one of the most powerful ways for brands to connect with their customers in the multi-channel, experience-oriented environment in which we live today.

Part I

Sponsors

CHAPTER 2

DEVELOPING SPONSORSHIP STRATEGY

Overview

This chapter looks at the process of creating a robust sponsorship strategy for a sponsor. The theory is discussed in some detail and is illustrated by case studies to demonstrate how that theory has been applied in practice.

This chapter covers:

- Why sponsorship strategy is important
- How to develop a sponsorship strategy for a sponsor organization
- Strategy in practice.

The strategy development process

According to research conducted by the European Sponsorship Association (ESA) the most important factor in achieving positive sponsorship outcomes is having a proper sponsorship strategy (see Figure 2.1).

It is important because a good strategy informs the decisions made about the types of sponsorships undertaken, the sorts of rights and benefits that need to be acquired from rights-holders, the focused allocation of limited resources when executing a sponsorship activation programme and, crucially, how success will be measured.

Both theory and practice suggests a six-step approach to developing a robust sponsorship strategy for a sponsor organization. These are:

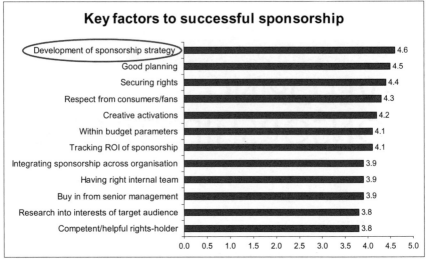

Source: European Sponsorship Association 2007

Figure 2.1 Key factors in successful sponsorship
(*Reproduced with permission of the European Sponsorship Association*)

1. Discovery
2. Development
3. Portfolio audit
4. Stress testing
5. Implementation
6. Review

1. Discovery

In order to create a good sponsorship strategy, a lot of data about an organization and the environment in which it operates needs to be gathered and analysed (see Figure 2.2).

(a) The brand

Central to an effective sponsorship strategy is a clear understanding of the organization's brand. The types of questions to ask are:

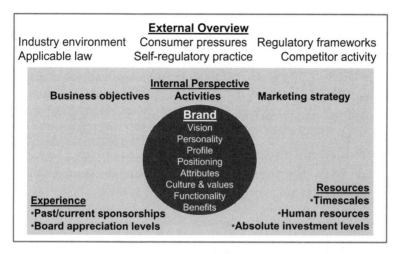

Figure 2.2 Developing sponsorship strategy: phase 1 – discovery

- What is the brand vision?
- What is its personality?
- What sort of profile does it have?
- How is it positioned in the marketplace, both against competitors and perhaps against other brands, big, small, niche, however they are positioned?
- What sort of attributes does the brand have?
- What are the culture and values of the brand and organization?
- What is the brand's functionality and, of course most importantly, the benefits that it gives to consumers?

(b) Internal environment

Having acquired a thorough understanding of the brand and its position, the wider internal perspective must be explored. This is divided into three elements:

Business focus

What are the main activities of the business, its short- and long-term objectives and priorities and what is the marketing strategy that is aimed at supporting achievement of these goals?

There is also a need to understand the organization's previous experience of sponsorship: What sponsorships have been undertaken in the past and to what extent were they successful? Is sponsorship being undertaken currently? What are people's impressions of those sponsorships and whether they are delivering, or not?

Of particular importance in sponsorship, owing to the size of the investment, is cognisance of how well the Board members understand sponsorship and appreciate it as a marketing discipline. Do they understand how sponsorship works or do they merely think it is an opportunity for them to have a decent hospitality ticket to something they want to see?

 Case Study: ECCO shoes

 Key learning points:

- Senior management need to disassociate their personal interests from sponsorship selection decisions.
- The best fit sponsorship opportunity may only be discovered after thorough research into the opportunities presented across the marketplace.

David Sleigh, the Managing Director of ECCO shoes, had absolute clarity on how sponsorship worked for his business, but also recognized the potential to de-rail ECCO's sponsorship activities by allowing his personal preference (rugby) to interfere with selecting a sponsorship that was relevant to the particular business challenge (targeting younger city worker women). He was absolutely determined that his personal interest should not be allowed to get in the way of making the best rational decision for the business. ECCO in fact eventually selected a sponsorship opportunity at the Victoria & Albert Museum that was wholly right for the brand, but about as far from rugby as one can get!

(With permission from David Sleigh)

Available resources

The most obvious resource-related questions revolve around absolute invest-ment levels that can be committed to paying rights fees for a sponsorship and then leveraging and evaluating it effectively. A sponsorship opportunity might appear to be very well suited for the business, but if the business is neither able nor willing to invest the appropriate amount in sponsorship, this needs to be clearly understood from the outset, allowing sponsorship decisions to be taken with this in mind. Specifically, there is no point in allowing an organization to sign up to – or believe it will optimize value out of – a significant investment in rights fees if there will not be enough financial support to leverage that investment through executing the best sponsorship activation programmes for the business's needs. Equally, there is little point in allowing an organization to invest heavily in a "trophy sponsorship" if other options are available that might achieve the same objectives, but at lower financial cost.

Less obvious, but perhaps more significant, is the question of what human resources might be made available to implement and manage a sponsorship programme? Will these be internal, or will external support be required? If the latter, where should the search start and what procurement regime must be respected?

Timing

Clarity around the sort of timescales the organization works with, and how these might impact sponsorship decisions, is critical. At one time fashion brands changed their collections twice a year; now the cycle for many has shortened to eight weeks. At the other end of the scale, the petrochemicals industry makes investments that may not be cash-positive for 40 years. The type of sponsorships that are relevant to each industry will be quite different.

(c) External perspective

As organizations do not exist in isolation, the external environment must be taken into account. Thinking again about the retail and petrochemicals indus-tries to illustrate the point: they operate in very different environments, appli-cable laws will differ by market, and the sorts of consumer pressures faced by the business or its competitors will also be different. Some industries are largely governed by self-regulatory practice; others more by significant and complex legislation. The competition's activities are also important. In some industries it may be appropriate to leverage widely different sponsorship platforms as a point of differentiation. For others, undertaking similar sponsorship may be perfectly acceptable, such as investment banking and art exhibitions. So it is not only what competitors are sponsoring, but whether sponsorship is perceived as a point of differentiation or a way of acquiring the same status that a competitor gained as a result of their sponsorship activity.

The discovery phase involves a lot of hard work. Some data will be available via desk research internally within the organization; the challenge is trying to identify relevant documents, gain access and synthesize the information. Further relevant data may also be available externally via the internet or reference libraries. Another excellent way of gathering information is through senior management interviews. Not only is it possible to gather real insights but also, by involving them in the strategy development process, there is less likelihood of their resistance to agreeing and implementing the final strategy. This is a critical issue and cannot be stressed strongly enough. If a new or revised sponsorship strategy is to have any hope of being properly implemented throughout the business, it will be very difficult to do if senior management are not absolutely on board with both the strategy itself and the need for a new strategy and a desire to make it happen within the organization.

Market research data is another valuable source of information. It may even be relevant to undertake some specific market research to answer key questions that perhaps the brand has not gathered historically in the context of sponsorship to ensure that the strategy is absolutely fit for purpose.

2. Strategy development

Having gathered all the data in the "discovery" phase it must be synthesized to create an initial draft of a new sponsorship strategy. An effective sponsorship strategy will cover the following:

- Rationale for sponsorship within the context of the organization and its corporate strategy.

- The role of sponsorship within the marketing mix: Whether sponsorship will be a strategic tool across the whole business at one end of the scale versus a desire to use it in a more tactical, targeted way. Illustrations of the former include Adidas and Red Bull, where the role of sponsorship is clearly viewed as strategically critical to business success.

- Top line objectives for sponsorship: Is sponsorship primarily aimed at creating value in the profit and loss account, through sponsorships with a clear line of sight to sales? Alternatively, is sponsorship largely to be deployed as a way of building brand equity and positively impacting the balance sheet? Perhaps the overall emphasis is to be on engaging with local communities and representing the organization as a good corporate citizen.

- The key target audience/s: For some organizations these will be quite broad; for others it might be more narrow in terms of which audiences they will target through sponsorship.

- Key deliverables: These focus on what the organization expects sponsorship to deliver. This could be many things but might include changes in brand metrics, positive sales impacts or share price movements, a higher quality of employment candidates or reduced churn among employees. A clear vision for sponsorship delivery will enable the organization to clarify the results that need to be achieved and therefore where resources need to be concentrated.

- The overall themes of sponsorship for the organization: The theme could be as broad as sport or engaging a specific key target audience. This is really to help the organization to think through what can be accepted as a sponsorship proposition and those items that actually fall outside the scope of the sponsorship strategy.

- Footprint and number of sponsorships: There is no point in securing sponsorships that have global appeal if the organization only operates in one market, as this will result in significant wastage. Equally, it is often perceived that a "global" sponsorship platform might work well for the majority of markets in which an organization operates, but there may be several markets where alternative opportunities will be more powerful in achieving objectives. If you are a global business then you may well wish to have a global sponsorship. If you are a single business in one market, spending money on a global sponsorship is wasteful unless you have big export ambitions. The optimum number of sponsorships will be very much about what sort of resources are to be made available in people management terms. Sponsorships, even if they are well managed, are quite hard work and are human resource intensive. If there are too many sponsorships, not only will the resources to manage them effectively be unavailable, but the outcome achievement will also be reduced. There will be little focus on achieving the best results as the emphasis will be mainly on "keeping all the plates spinning". The discussion internally will always focus on the highest level of local market relevance, with the perception of an associated maximization of outcomes, versus the economies of scale offered by a global platform. There is no "right" answer to this question and each organization will need to think this through carefully in the context of its own operating environment.

- Timeframes for review: It is very important to have a timeframe for strategy reviews. This should directly reflect the timeframes in which the business operates.
- Role of current sponsorships: Before a new sponsorship strategy can be fully agreed, whether and how any current sponsorships fit with the new approach needs careful consideration. This is largely addressed in phase 3 of sponsorship strategy development, the Portfolio Audit.

 Case Study: Global financial services brand

 Key learning points:

- The clear definition of targets – both audiences and objectives – are critical to sponsorship success.

continued on next page...

- A sponsorship strategy does not necessarily dictate exactly what should be sponsored – rather it provides guidance that can be adapted to local market circumstances.

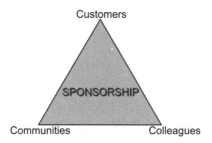

Figure 2.3 The organization's sponsorship target audiences

This global financial services firm recognized that it was investing in a large number of sponsorships around the globe in support of its business interests, but felt that it needed a more robust strategy to guide local markets in selecting specific sponsorship projects. Through a review process it identified the key target audiences for sponsorship, as illustrated in Figure 2.3.

The main target audience was defined as customers and involving customers in the activities of the firm, but there was also a very strong strand that focused on communities. Sponsorship was used to contribute to communities, particularly in terms of engaging with other thought leaders and stakeholders in the locality. Thirdly, and unsurprisingly with an organization of this size, sponsorships were also targeted at impacting colleagues with the aim of improving employees' perceptions of the firm as an attractive employer. The organization then defined the sources of value it expected sponsorship investments to deliver in terms of a positive impact on the brand and/or the business itself as:

continued on next page ...

- Business generation
- Brand reputation
- Brand exposure
- Internal engagement
- Direct business
- Spectator experience
- Personal financial services sales

The firm sees sponsorship as a very flexible marketing tool which can be activated in different ways to meet specific market challenges. It is important to them to have clarity around sponsorship objectives so that each sponsorship is activated in the right way and is given the correct budget. Not only that, but clear objectives also ensure that the way each sponsorship's activation budget is apportioned is focused on making the sponsorship come alive to deliver on its specific objectives. The firm has melded together the various strands of its sponsorship strategy into a defined vision for sponsorship:

> "We are committed to engaging the next generation through experiences in sports and arts around the world, developing values for life that reflect [our] vision and values."

The sponsorship vision is based on connecting with young people and providing consistency throughout the portfolio of sponsorships. The vision is the consistent thread that is woven through the activation of the firm's sponsorships and focuses on developing youth, furthering education and embracing communities in some or all of their sponsorship activation. In essence, the vision is very much based on connecting with young people, the next generation of customers, through stimulating sports and arts activities. The vision, however, does not dictate what to sponsor or how to sponsor, but it is a consistent approach for a stream of activation that adds value to stakeholders and the brand. Now over 80% of the firm's local sponsorships are activated with an element of youth, education and community.

The sponsorship policy

The other resource that is key to successful strategy deployment is having a clearly defined sponsorship policy. The sponsorship policy is rather more focused on the managerial aspects of the sponsorship strategy. This includes details of the different roles involved from: (a) who will actually be responsible for running the sponsorships? (b) who are the decision makers; (c) who are the supporters; to (d) who will actually implement each sponsorship undertaken?

The policy will also contain guidelines around how to select a sponsorship – for example: a list of which sponsorship benefits should be included in any sponsorship agreement. If the sponsor is primarily looking at business-to-business engagement, then entertaining will be important. If the focus is more on building the brand then opportunities for branding and creating brand awareness will be more critical to the company, and these are described here.

The whole issue of money should also be covered within the sponsorship policy; this includes the way sponsorships will be funded from within a corporation, which is often a key issue. The extent to which there is a preference for offering value in kind or marketing in kind instead of, or in tandem with, a cash payment should also be communicated. Value in kind could be the provision of technology or skills that are an important part of the offer that the organization might make to rights-holders. Marketing in kind can also be valuable to a rights-holder if the sponsor is able to amplify the property's own marketing efforts in relevant channels.

The extent to which sponsorship or category exclusivity is relevant should also be addressed. For some businesses total "ownership" of the sponsorship is important to ensure that only their brand is associated with the property and only they have access to the property's benefits. Other corporations may actively seek multi-sponsor opportunities as a way of building their own brand stature by being seen in quality company.

The corporation may also stipulate certain exclusions or restrictions that will influence sponsorship selection or activation. Some brands might not wish to sponsor individuals, perceiving them as too high a risk. Others might choose not to sponsor activities where there was a relatively high risk of injury to participants and spectators. Many corporations stipulate that they will not sponsor anything that is discriminatory, in support of their wider Inclusion and Diversity policies.

The policy will detail the steps in the company's sponsorship selection process and determine who is to be involved in selection decisions. It is critically important to establish the criteria that will be used to assess sponsorship proposals. Clearly defined criteria are also useful because they help to remove emotion from the sponsorship assessment and selection process. Further information on sponsorship selection can be found in Chapter 3.

Finally, the sponsorship policy should establish how sponsorship outcomes will be evaluated, describing the kind of data that will need to be collected and reviewed, the processes that will need to be conducted, the timing and regularity or reviews, and who will be responsible for reviewing and reporting results.

 ## 3. Portfolio audit

Having created the initial drafts of the sponsorship strategy and sponsorship policy, the next step is to understand the impact of the proposed strategy on any current sponsorships. A simple tool to assist in this is a four-box matrix, as illustrated in Figure 2.4.

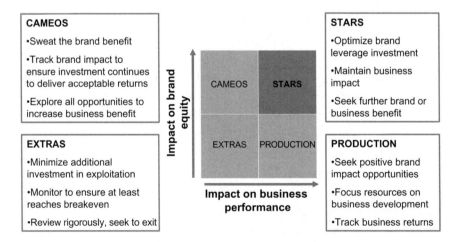

Figure 2.4 Portfolio audit matrix

The horizontal or x axis tracks the impact on business performance – that is, how a sponsorship is performing in terms of delivering positive bottom-line impact. The vertical or y axis measures impact on building brand equity which translates into value created in the corporation's balance sheet.

Stars

Stars are those sponsorships that are delivering strongly on both business performance and building brand equity and will continue to do so within the framework of the proposed new strategy. The focus going forward will be on investing in leveraging the brand benefits and ensuring that positive business impact is maintained or even increased.

Extras

At the other end of the scale the "extras" can be found. These are the sponsorships that will be weak performers under the new strategy. Decisions will need to be made about minimizing investment and exploitation. Focus will need to be on doing the minimum necessary for these sponsorships to break even while planning how to exit elegantly.

Cameos

Cameo sponsorships are those that will deliver strongly against building brand equity under the proposed sponsorship strategy, but have less impact on the bottom line. Retaining these sponsorships is fine as long as they continue to deliver brand benefits, but all opportunities to increase their business performance should be explored.

Production

These are the workhorses of the sponsorship portfolio, which will continue to produce lots of money under the proposed strategy but may not be perceived as very exciting. Resources should be focused on maintaining their business performance, with some effort expended to identify ways to increase their brand contribution.

4. Stress-testing

Once you are satisfied that the proposed strategy has taken into account any current sponsorships and that the likely outcomes of adopting the strategy for the organization are understood, the next step is to stress-test the new strategy with a wider audience.

Internally the draft strategy should be reviewed with key personnel. Here you are looking to identify areas of resistance, whether the feeling is neutral or indeed if it is perceived as well fit-for-purpose. Initial resistance should not be viewed negatively but as an opportunity to surface and resolve any major issues, or indeed minor ones, that can be fixed fairly easily. Equally, you may find that you have crafted something that is absolutely brilliant but did not yet know that senior management are planning to take the business in a wholly different direction.

Internal stress-testing also presents opportunities to identify any misconceptions. There might be a lack of understanding around sponsorship, its role and application, or there might be misconceptions around the whole strategy review. Stress-testing should be viewed as a way to draw people into the process, to let their voices be heard, to deal with their issues in a useful and positive way, and at least to identify who your enemies might be as you go forward. It also helps to define the success criteria that should be adopted when implementing this new strategy.

Having gathered internal perspectives and refined the strategy accordingly, you may also want to look at how this strategy will impact externally before it is implemented. One way of doing this is to undertake research among key target audiences to understand whether they will appreciate the new direction going forward, or whether it might make them antagonistic towards the brand. This research is likely to be some focus group work rather than a big quantitative study, allowing you to be able to delve really deeply into how people feel while keeping it fairly narrow in terms of the number who are exposed to your thought process to maintain confidentiality. Even if the process is quite informal, the research will highlight any major concerns among key target audiences and may generate some really valuable insights from customers and other stakeholders into how you might actually increase the positive impact of the new strategy. Customers in particular often have a very authentic perspective of a brand, with some good ideas about what could be done better.

5. Implementation

Once you are fully satisfied that the strategy will work and that implementation risks have been minimized through stress-testing, the first step in successful implementation is to embark on a robust internal selling-in programme. You will then need to think about how to exit from sponsorships that are no longer supported by the strategy, and communicate the new strategy externally where relevant.

Externally it may be appropriate to make a "big splash" and announce that there is a new strategic sponsorship direction. At other times, especially if you may be accused of cutting back on investment in sponsorship, it may be better to simply allow the new strategy to settle into place without making it highly visible.

Where gaps in the sponsorship portfolio have been identified in terms of achieving key business objectives, now is the time to start the search and selection process. This may take longer than you imagine as, rather like human resources recruitment, conducting a wide-ranging process to ensure that a broad cross-section of opportunities is reviewed will inevitably require an investment in time to find best-fit solutions.

6. Review

Implementing a new strategy is both exciting and challenging but it is also very important to remember to review that strategy periodically. The purpose is to check how well the strategy is delivering, whether the business has moved on in the meantime and whether the strategy is therefore still fit for purpose. The result may be that it must be refined or completely reconstructed in the light of new business imperatives.

Prior to a formal review, gathering informal responses internally on how key influencers think the strategy is working will be invaluable in achieving successful outcomes. Collect data in terms of the established success criteria and how you are expected to measure performance, and make sure that results are reported. Along the way, opportunities for improving, tailoring or subtly shifting the strategy to deliver greater benefit may become apparent.

The frequency of reviews will have been identified in the overall strategy-setting process. A full review at any particular milestones that were defined in the strategy should be conducted to make sure that it continues to deliver brand and business results. Roughly speaking, depending on the cycle time of the business, a full review should be conducted, on average, once every three to five years. Alternatively, it may be driven by a major sponsorship coming up for renewal, and this will be the appropriate timeframe if the organization has adopted a single sponsorship strategy.

 Case Study: Strategy Review

 Key learning points

- Strategy reviews may need to be conducted sooner than planned on a regular cycle as a result of some major change internally within an organization or externally in the environment in which the company operates.
- Strategy reviews do not necessarily mean cutting sponsorships, but they support the organization in taking a disciplined approach to sponsorship investments.

In 2005 when Siemens sold its mobile division to BenQ, it also lost its shirt sponsorship of football club Real Madrid. This resulted in reduced brand visibility which led Siemens plc to reassess its approach to sponsorship.

The discovery phase involved:

- Research to identify what sponsorships were used by competitors and how these were leveraged to create value.

continued on next page ...

- An exhaustive interview process involving senior management across all senior personnel in 22 UK divisions on Siemens' activities, decision-making processes and aspirations.

From this activity Siemens developed a sponsorship strategy that was based on a portfolio approach. This balanced a London focus with regional reach to resonate with all Siemens' UK businesses. The strategy also distilled six key sponsorship objectives and devised an associated decision-making framework to guide future investments.

The outcome of this process was a series of award-winning sponsorships including an ongoing relationship with the Science Museum, London (including touring exhibitions) a record-breaking six year relationship with GB Rowing, The Big Bang Young Scientists and Engineers Fair in Manchester and, more recently, an announcement of a new international sponsorship of the Academy of St Martin in the Fields, London.

(Reproduced with permission of Siemens plc)

Conclusion

One issue with creating and implementing a robust sponsorship strategy is whether it is really worth the effort required. The main argument in favour of developing a strategy is that alignment and a focus on contributing to longer term goals means that sponsorship becomes much more embedded in the organization, more relevant and better appreciated as a marketing discipline. Having a documented strategy also gives new managers with sponsorship responsibilities the opportunity to understand what it was that the organization was trying to achieve when this strategy was set to enable them to evaluate whether key objectives have been delivered and the strategy's continued fitness-for-purpose.

With sponsorship policy, clarifying the company's position to the external market should have the benefit of reducing the number of speculative approaches that are not on target for the business. It makes the assessment of proposals easier and rejections to be unequivocal where opportunities do not meet the policy's selection criteria.

 ## Key take-outs

- Senior management support is essential to developing and implementing a new sponsorship strategy. Without them it will be very difficult to gain traction for the strategy across the organization. People generally like the status quo and dislike change and, particularly in sponsorship terms, there may be senior managers with vested interests in certain pet projects that the new strategy identifies as underperformers. The sponsorship manager alone will not be effective in these circumstances.
- Sponsorship strategy is not a project which, once completed, can be filed away. It is a dynamic activity, an iterative process, and its elements need to be reviewed regularly. That may not mean monthly, but reviews should be aligned with the frequency with which your business changes.
- A robust sponsorship strategy facilitates alignment, whether that is within the sponsorship department, the marketing team, across other departments, other divisions or markets.

Summary

A robust sponsorship strategy is widely accepted as the key to sponsorship success because it informs selection decisions, directs execution spend towards activities that focus on achievement of objectives, and highlights the key performance indicators that should be tracked to provide a report on sponsorship success.

CHAPTER 3

PLANNING FOR SUCCESS

 ## Overview

This chapter focuses on the sponsorship selection process. Having developed the sponsorship strategy and identified that sponsorship is the right approach for the organization, the next step is to transform that strategy into actionable plans that culminate in researching, selecting and negotiating the right sponsorship(s) to fit the organization's brand business and needs. This chapter covers:

- Sponsorship selection criteria and selection mechanisms
- Acquiring the appropriate rights
- Different ways of paying for rights
- Some issues around contracting
- Dealing with the "Chairman's whim"
- Common mistakes in sponsorship selection and how to avoid them

 ## The planning process

Over 150 years ago Abraham Lincoln emphasized the importance of good planning when he said:

> "If I had eight hours to cut down a tree, I would spend six hours sharpening the saw."

Planning is no less important in sponsorship, and developing a robust sponsorship plan is recognized as the second most important factor in delivering successful sponsorship in the European Sponsorship Association Survey 2007 (see Figure 2.1).

Establishing the need for a new sponsorship

Planning in the context of the sponsorship process begins with establishing whether a new sponsorship is essential to achieve the desired outcomes (see Figure 3.1).

As discussed in Chapter 2, sponsorship strategy is derived from the marketing and business strategy which will identify the key target audiences in terms of their socio-demographics, their personal interests and the sort of priorities that are relevant to their lives. The overall business strategy will have various objectives, whether they are related to building the brand, more commercially oriented or softer objectives around engaging with key stakeholders such as government or NGOs.

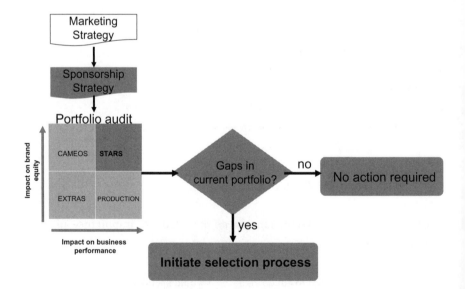

Figure 3.1 Establishing the need for a new sponsorship

Once sure of the overall strategy, the current portfolio of sponsorships needs to be reviewed to identify whether there are any underperforming properties that should be exited and also whether there are opportunities to sweat certain sponsorships further to achieve desired goals. It may be that "cameo" or "production" sponsorships can be worked harder to make them "stars" rather than simply going out and buying something new to solve a particular problem. Only if gaps in the portfolio are identified should a sponsorship selection process be initiated.

Agree selection criteria

Before starting a search process, the first thing needed is to agree the selection criteria against which possible sponsorships will be judged and compared. Some of the things that might be considered are given below.

? Sponsorship selection criteria

The level of "ownership" required of a property in order to achieve the defined sponsorship objectives.
- Do you perhaps want to be a supplier to a property because it fits your objectives of showcasing your products and services?
- You might want to be in a multi-sponsor environment adding to your corporate status by being seen to be in good quality company. A good example is the Corporate Partners Programme at the British Museum.

How exploitable does the partnership need to be?
- This depends very much on your objectives.
- If it is primarily a business-to-business hospitality opportunity, the main requirement will be to entice key audiences to attend hosted events, while property advertising is only relevant to the extent that it enhances the perception of the exclusivity of the opportunity.
- A global consumer-oriented product will need a sponsorship that can be campaigned in a variety of ways to meet the slightly differing needs of different markets.

Geographic footprint of sponsorship
- There is no point in having a multi-national sponsorship if the sponsor's business operates in only one market, unless the objective of sponsoring a multi-national event is to create the perception that the sponsor's organization is perhaps stronger than it is in reality.
- A good example is UK-based bank Lloyds TSB which chose to be a sponsor of The London Organizing Committee for the Olympic Games rather than partner the International Olympic Committee because the bank has no customers outside the UK.

Rights and benefits available
- What assets are essential for the sponsorship to be effective and what benefits are merely nice to have available?
- There may be some other useful rights that the rights-holder has not yet offered that are highly relevant to your particular sponsorship objectives.

Sponsorship property SWOT analysis (Strengths, Weaknesses, Opportunities and Threats)
- This would include macro-analysis when looking at threats like terrorism, hostile NGOs, legislation, etc.

Evaluation data availability
- This will depend on key performance indicators.
- See what sort of data the rights-holder already has available that might be of use. For example, savings could be made if they have data they share with co-sponsors.

Quality of the rights-holder
- One of the best guides to this is a rights-holder's track record in looking after their sponsors and, crucially, retaining them over time.
- However, there may be times when a brand has to be prepared to take a risk on an untried and untested rights-holder. For example, the development of extreme sports has provided an ideal platform for some brands but was initially organized by non-traditional rights-holders.

Anticipated ROI and ROO
- At some point somebody senior in the sponsor's organization is likely to ask what anticipated returns will be, whether that is in terms of return on investment (ROI) or return on objectives (ROO).
- Establishing a "hurdle" rate of return and modelling outcomes to give an indication of returns in conservative and aggressive scenarios will assist considerably in comparing different sponsorship opportunities.

Outline activation plan
- As part of the selection process an outline activation plan should be created in order to compare potential exploitability and, therefore, which sponsorships are going to give the most scope to achieve the desired outcome.

Primary/secondary validation research
- There may be primary research that says that particular types of properties will be more relevant to the brand. Alternatively, there may be a simple requirement to see some research that gives an indication of the demographics of the target property and how well those match with the sponsor's target audience demographics.

Practical parameters

These selection criteria have necessarily to be balanced against some fairly practical parameters.

- *Budget* – How much money is to be made available for the purchase and leverage of sponsorship rights?
- *People* – What sort of people will be needed to implement the sponsorship effectively, and are they accessible, including operations, advertising, PR, sales promotions, etc.
- *Timeframes* – These can be used to make selection and implementation decisions.
- *Specific exclusions* – These may relate to a preference for not sponsoring individuals or particular types of activities, such as avoiding dangerous sports like motor racing.

Research properties

Only once the selection criteria have been agreed can the sponsorship search begin. The challenge is to remain open-minded and explore a variety of opportunities across the spectrum of sponsorship possibilities listed in Chapter 1.

Added to all those possibilities is the increasing trend of "DIY" sponsorship properties. This is where there is no existing property that really meets the needs of the brand, and where the brand has the appetite and resources to create its own sponsorship property – for example, the Red Bull Air Race, which is self-owned. This has been very successful strategy for Red Bull but brands must remember to focus on what is core to their business. Creating and establishing a new property is going to drain resources from the organization. Therefore, a thorough risk/reward analysis should be undertaken to check that the proposition will not overly burden the organization and potentially damage primary revenue sources as a result.

Sponsorship assessment methodologies

Having researched possible properties, the next step is to screen them against any exclusion criteria and then assess them against the predetermined selection criteria to develop a shortlist of the highest potential opportunities. Owing to the amount of analysis that will need to be undertaken before a final decision can be made, it is recommended that the shortlist should be no more than five properties, with only three being preferable. When the shortlist has been agreed there are various methods of assessing each sponsorship in order to make comparisons between the various properties, of which four are discussed below.

1. Decision trees

Where the selection criteria are relatively straightforward, and the type of property well understood by the organization, it may be possible to develop a decision tree by creating a series of questions with yes/no answers to guide decision making.

Case Study: Broadcast Sponsorship Decision Tree

 Key learning points:

- Some sponsorship selection decisions can be made by developing easy to use, time saving and transparent ways of reaching decisions.
- These also have the benefit of transcending cultural differences for brands operating across national borders.

Especially in sport, but occasionally in cultural sponsorship, there is both the opportunity and pressure to sponsor the broadcast feed relating to a sponsored activity in one or more markets. This may lead to an incoherent strategy with broadcast sponsorship being undertaken arbitrarily in some markets but not in others. One brand tackled this issue by creating a decision tree to help local business managers decide whether investing in sponsorship-related broadcast sponsorship was appropriate for each market.

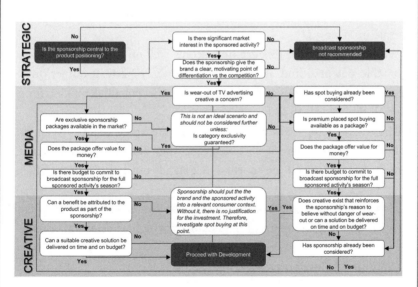

Figure 3.2 Broadcast sponsorship decision tree

Table 3.1 Example of the absolute score methodology

Criteria	Property A Score out of 10	Property B Score out if 10
Amount of global brand exposure	8	6
Match between property brand attributes and the sponsor's brand	6	9
Staff engagement opportunities	4	8
Exploitable potential in sponsorship opportunity for the brand	8	7
Attractiveness of hospitality to our target audiences	8	6
Business generation potential	6	9
Total Score	40	45

2. Absolute score against selection criteria

This methodology is perhaps the most simple to create, in that each predetermined selection criterion is scored out of 5 or 10, or some other preferred number, with the final scores added together to provide the data for direct comparison between different properties, as illustrated in the fictitious example in Table 3.1.

While Property A in this example scores well on global brand exposure, exploitable potential and attractive hospitality, Property B outperforms on matching brand attributes and business generation potential, making Property B overall the better option for the sponsor.

This methodology is suitable for where the sponsorship investment is relatively small or where it becomes clear that, following further research, there is one property on the shortlist that stands out well above the others as the preferred option.

However, more significant and/or complex investment decisions might be better informed using the third methodology: weighted selection criteria.

3. Weighted selection criteria

The starting point for the weighted selection criteria methodology is similar to that in Table 3.1 and is usually easiest to deploy using a computer spreadsheet.

Then, rather than allocate the same maximum score to each criterion, either different maximum scores are given or a multiplier is applied to differentiate those criteria that carry the most importance in the decision-making process. This is a system that has historically been used by a multi-national mobile telecoms brand to guide their sponsorship selection decisions.

 Case Study: Multi-National Mobile Telecoms Brand

 Key learning points:

- Weighting the scores emphasizes those criteria that are most important in the selection process.
- Weighting of selection criteria can easily be changed to meet new market circumstances.

This example illustrated overleaf shows that the criteria for this brand are: brand equity building and creating awareness, opportunities for corporate social responsibility, employee motivation, managing relationships, demonstrating their products, or indeed even getting trials for them, providing some unique content followed by sales support and some sort of integration platform.

The box on the extreme right-hand side of Figure 3.3 shows that, at the time this particular weighting was in use, the most important criterion for the company was brand equity building, followed by creating brand awareness. Brand equity building would probably be relatively less heavily weighted now because mobile telecoms' brands, certainly in Europe, have matured and their focus now is on gaining market share.

The result of all this is a chart (Figure 3.4). The columns in the figure represent the relative weightings of the brand's sponsorship selection criteria. The line shows how well a particular sponsorship scored against the weighted criteria. While this project gained an overall score of 81%, which would be considered a good fit, it is only by looking into the specifics that the real picture emerges.

continued on next page ...

Prioritization of Role		Ranking with %
Please rank the 9 roles relative to each other in order of importance: (Scale: 1 = top priority; 9 = bottom	No.	100%
Brand Equity Building	1	26%
Brand Awareness	2	15%
CSR	5	10%
Employee Motivation	9	2%
Relationship Management	3	14%
Product Demonstration/Trial	4	13%
Unique Content	6	9%
Support Sales	7	8%
Integration Platform	8	3%

Figure 3.3 Weighted sponsorship selection criteria

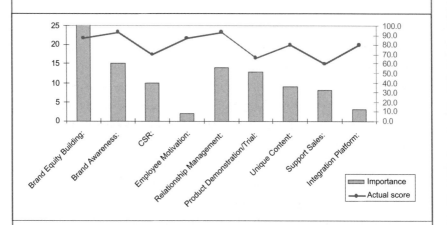

Figure 3.4 Illustration of outcomes from weighted criteria

This project scored well on brand equity building, but there were also some high points around "Employee motivation" and "Integrated platform" which, at the time, were relatively unimportant to the company. In fact, the property overall slightly under-scored on the most important criterion of brand equity building, and rather over-scored on virtually everything else, with only the product demonstration/trial criterion coming the closest to the company's weighted requirements.

This methodology can be applied to determine sponsorship investment decisions or it can be used as the source for internal debate to look at how a better fit can be created between a proposed sponsorship and an organization's specific requirements.

4. Qualitative judgement

This methodology involves a more qualitative assessment of a property's fit with the sponsor's needs.

 Case Study: Global Financial Services Firm

 Key learning points:

- Simple pre-screening filters out irrelevant proposals to reduce the burden of assessment on the sponsor's organization.
- Qualitative assessment does not exclude the need to create success metrics prior to a sponsorship decision being made.

This firm uses a three-stage approach to sponsorship assessment:

- Stage 1 involves pre-screening of all sponsorship proposals received to eliminate all those that cannot meet the firm's key criteria. This ensures that resources are expended only on considering those opportunities that have the highest potential for the organization.
- Stage 2 requires a qualitative evaluation looking first at whether a particular sponsorship fits with the organization's strategic criteria, such as fit with vision and values, target audiences and business objectives. Without a compelling proposition at the strategic level

continued on next page ...

there is little point in investing resources to investigate the opportunity further.

- Stage 3 requires a full assessment where a property is taken through an evaluation framework of six issues, one of which focuses on post-investment evaluation. These include: (a) the objectives the sponsorship will meet, (b) the key target audiences that will be reached, and (c) the metrics that will be presented to demonstrate how a sponsorship has shifted behaviour or thoughts on the brand. For example, if, say, the firm had an objective about creating awareness among ABC1 men, then the metrics would be brand awareness scores from their brand tracker. It is then possible to define success in terms of a defined rise in percentage brand awareness globally among this key target audience.

5. Gut feel!

It may be laughable, but if really good brand managers are finely attuned to the needs of their brand and the corporation, intuition will take them a long way in the sponsorship selection process. Although the sponsorship industry jokes about "Chairman's whim" and vanity sponsorships, some of these can be absolutely on target for their organization if they are selected with the same intuition that led the founder to brand and business success.

Therefore, those responsible for sponsorship investment decisions should still listen to what resonates with the organization's brand and business managers. Think hard about projects that feel right because they may just be completely on target, in which case a lot of time and effort can be saved by not having to develop and implement detailed screening and assessment processes.

Negotiating the right deal

As discussed in Chapter 1, it is important to remember that the perspective of the sponsor and rights-holder may be completely different and awareness of this is critical to conducting an effective sponsorship negotiation. It also means that sponsors and rights-holders may perceive value in different things, allowing both parties to make trade-offs that assist the negotiation process to conclude with a win–win result.

Sponsors should make use of all resources available to them to secure the best arrangement for their particular needs, and specifically the right human resources, including representation from commercial, procurement, legal and HR. They will be invaluable in bringing different perspectives and experiences to the negotiating table that will enhance the final outcome on behalf of the sponsor. The negotiating team is then in a position to determine exactly what rights the rights-holder is selling, which might include:

- Branding and livery on some or all of the rights-holder's, collateral
- Use of the rights-holder's marks and logos to promote the association
- Naming rights to the sponsored buildings, vehicles, events, etc.
- The right to produce, use or sell licensed merchandise
- The right to distribute products or provide services to attendees
- The ability to provide products or services on the "field of play", such as soft drinks at half time, the sound system for a concert or product placement in a movie
- Endorsement of the sponsor's products or services by relevant employees of the rights-holder's organization
- The right to use the sponsored activity in a sponsor's sales promotion plans
- An expectation that the rights-holder will work hard to promote the association and get the sponsor mentioned in the media, including online
- A number of personal appearances by the key players in the rights-holder's organization, usually the 'stars' of the show, but may include senior management or operations staff depending on the sponsor's product/service set
- The promise that the rights-holder will not allow a competitor to become a sponsor and promote the same products or services as defined in the original sponsor's contract – known as category exclusivity
- Access to a predetermined number of tickets for the sponsored activity where relevant

- Defined hospitality and venue usage both during the sponsored activity and, if available, for the sponsor to hold other meetings and events for its own purposes
- Database access to allow the sponsor to promote its association with the sponsored activity and its products or services to those with an interest in the rights-holder's activities.

It is in a rights-holder's interest to package assets so that they sell some of what they perceive as the less attractive rights linked with those that are more attractive as a way of increasing the package value and, therefore, the sponsorship fees demanded. However, much of a package being offered may not be very relevant to achieving the sponsors' objectives and therefore they will need to negotiate on the rights they desire to 'cherry pick' from different packages on offer from the rights-holder, as illustrated in Figure 3.5.

For example, if it is the hospitality opportunity for business entertaining that attracts the organization, it may not need the pitch-side branding that the rights-holder considers to be very valuable and is therefore selling the package at a high price. Equally, the organization may not need much top-end hospitality when a lot of this is included in the package, but just a few standard tickets for what is primarily a sales-promotion-related purchase for the sponsor.

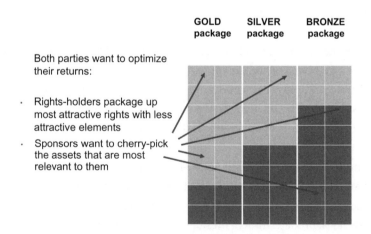

Figure 3.5 Optimizing the benefits package

The secret to identifying the correct rights for the sponsor's specific needs is to take a bottom-up approach. Once it is clear what the rights-holder can offer, the sponsor should discuss the potential assets with all relevant departments to determine those assets that will have the most use and value for the organization, and those that will not be used. Some of the assets that were originally deemed to be highly relevant, and have high cost, may be found to be less essential than others being offered. Also, departments may identify completely new assets from which they would be able to derive value that can then be presented to the rights-holder for discussion.

Unfortunately, being absolutely sure what rights the rights-holder is, and is not, selling answers only one of the key questions a sponsor needs to know before actually signing a contract. There are other significant questions that the sponsor needs to address.

⑦ Key questions

1. What are the obligations to the sponsor and does the rights-holder have the resources to deliver these effectively?
2. What are the rights-holder's obligations, if any, to help the sponsor to deliver on the specific sponsorship objectives?
3. How can the sponsor protect its investment, and what contingency plans are in place, or methods of redress, should the sponsorship not be delivered as envisaged, including:
   - What happens around ambush marketing and how can both sponsor and rights-holder work together to protect against it?
   - What can be done to plan for, and ameliorate, acts of God?
   - How does the sponsor legislate for deliberate misconduct by the rights-holder, whether that is negligence by the rights-holder or even strike action by their players, performers or management?
4. What are the sponsor's rights of renewal, including first refusal, and on what basis might renewal be refused by the rights-holder?
5. To what extent will the rights-holder be flexible during the term of the sponsorship if the sponsor's business circumstances change?
6. What legislation applies to the rights-holder's activities and is there, as a minimum, satisfactory evidence that the rights-holder is compliant?

Only when a sponsor is satisfied on all these issues should they embark on a discussion of fees and other value to be delivered to the rights-holder, otherwise known as 'consideration'.

Contract consideration: a balancing act

Consideration is a legal term and it is the price that one pays for acquiring the rights of association for entering into a contract. There are two sorts of consideration, cash and non-cash, as illustrated in Figure 3.6.

Cash as a type of consideration is the most common and comes in the form of the sponsorship fee. This is either paid in advance of the sponsored activity, where the activity is of short duration, or structured as scheduled payments over the lifetime of a longer term sponsorship. Sometimes performance bonuses are included, usually based around sports performance such as wins or number of goals.

While many rights-holders largely prefer cash as consideration because it allows them the flexibility to allocate it where they wish, there is a lot of other value that can potentially be given by the sponsor in exchange for the rights of association and other benefits. As illustrated in Figure 3.6, *value in kind* might include providing personnel, materials, technology or specialist skills.

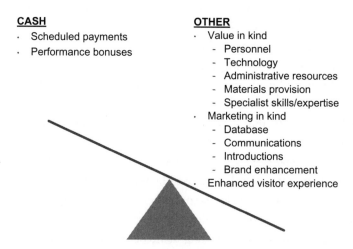

Figure 3.6 Possible types of consideration in a sponsorship contract

Marketing in kind might be achieved by amplifying the rights-holder's own marketing budget through the sponsor's marketing activities or by enhancing the visitor/fan experience in some way.

Value or marketing in kind is an attractive option for sponsors because it may reduce the total cost of the partnership by offsetting some of the hard cash requirement against benefits that have a high perceived value to the rights-holder but a much lower cost to deliver for the sponsor. Non-cash consideration is also beneficial to the sponsor because it helps to create the perception of a more authentic and credible relationship with the rights-holder, as viewed by the sponsored activity's fans.

Contracting

The authors have no pretensions to being legally trained and therefore the information below is meant only as a guide. Based on their own experience, they recommend strongly that all sponsorship negotiations and contracts are drawn up using legal representation that has a track record in the particular field. Negotiating a sponsorship contract may be perceived as more interesting than some of the other work corporate lawyers are asked to undertake, but unless they are already highly experienced in this field, there are too many opportunities for them to miss something critical when working in a field for which they have no accurate frame of reference.

The essentials of a sponsorship contract will include clauses that cover the terms laid out in Table 3.2.

Legal and regulatory frameworks

As highlighted in Chapter 2, sponsorship relationships do not exist in isolation and particular attention should be paid to the legal and regulatory frameworks that apply to a particular relationship. These may pertain not only to the home markets in which the sponsor and rights-holder are registered, but also to those governing the sponsorship in any other markets where the sponsored activity occurs or in which it is activated by the sponsor.

While these will vary around the world, the types of legislation that may need to be taken into account include:

Table 3.2 Essential sponsorship contract terms

Essential sponsorship contract terms	
Offer and acceptance	Deliverables by both parties + service level
Term	agreements
Identity of contractual parties	Responsibilities and obligations of the parties
Consideration	Rights protection (copyright, unfair
Territories	competition, database rights)
Exclusivity	Force majeure
Costs and VAT/sales tax application	Termination
	"Boilerplate": liabilities, arbitration,
	applicable law, etc.

- Privacy
- Communications, especially Electronic Communications
- Copyright
- Trademarks
- Image rights
- Ambush marketing
- Ticketing terms and conditions
- Marketing to children
- Sales promotion

Again, specific sponsorship legal advisers rather than in-house lawyers should be able to identify key pieces of legislation and other rules that need to be taken into account in the context of the proposed sponsorship relationship.

Other considerations

Other considerations that sponsors should take into account during the contracting process are:

(1) *Timing*
Drawing up contracts always takes much longer than expected. If the time available is limited by the timetable of the sponsored activity, the sponsor needs to think very carefully before finalizing a contract because of the risks

of unfortunate consequences from a contract negotiated without the time for due thought and investigation. Therefore, for a robust negotiation to be conducted, it is important for the sponsor to plan in plenty of time and start as early as possible.

(2) Pro forma contracts

Unless they are a completely new rights-holder, the likelihood is that they will already have one or more sponsorship contracts in place. Sponsors should therefore ask the rights-holder for their pro forma as this should:

- identify the skeleton of the contract onto which the sponsor's particular needs can be crafted;
- raise any unexplored issues relating to the sponsored activity that can then be discussed;
- reduce the sponsor's legal costs as lawyers are not required to draft the contract from scratch.

(3) Be prepared to negotiate on every word

Often agreeing the legal details of the contract gives rise to questions about the commercial terms already negotiated. It is important that these are revisited to ensure that the final contract terms are all aligned and reflect the full agreement between the parties.

(4) Populate the schedules and appendices prior to signature

Many contracts are signed without the schedules being properly completed. Then, when a dispute arises at a later date, the contract is inconclusive due to the lack of information in the schedules. It is therefore a critical discipline to insist on fully populated schedules, particularly with regard to how branding will appear, prior to signature.

(5) Service level agreements and performance measures

Sponsorship contracts usually clearly define deliverables in terms of rights and consideration, but fail to address process issues and performance requirements with the same vigour. Agreeing processes for raising and resolving issues and disputes, and the regularity and content of performance reviews, is good business practice.

(6) *Put the contract away until the sponsorship is up for review*
One of the advantages of a thorough contracting process is that the debate it creates helps both the sponsor and the rights-holder to better understand the other's organization, perspectives, priorities and success factors. This allows both parties much more flexibility throughout the contract term to adhere to and support the spirit of the relationship as well as meeting their immediate contractual obligations.

Sponsorship selection errors and remedies

While this chapter has tried to provide a 'bullet-proof' process for selecting sponsorships that will have successful outcomes for an organization, there are times when issues may arise that are largely outside the control of the sponsorship manager.

Choosing the wrong sponsorship

This is normally the result of either basing sponsorship selection decisions on emotional rather than rational considerations or as a result of a genuine error of judgement.

There are three ways in which emotions can cloud sponsorship selection decisions:

1. *Decisions are based on personal interests rather than rational data.* These emotional decisions can be senior management preferences or Chairman's wife syndrome – she likes opera therefore the organization invests in sponsoring opera, however inappropriate for the needs of the business. Another alternative is that somebody senior in a rights-holder went to school with somebody senior in a major corporation, and they now think it would be fun to revive their relationship through a sponsorship.
2. *The lure of glamour.* Being associated with something exciting and being able to mix with celebrities or attend prestigious events is important to some individuals and can influence which sponsorships they favour.

3. *Corporate emotional baggage.* A sponsor with a long association with a particular activity may find it hard to recognize when a sponsorship is no longer fit-for-purpose. They therefore renew without really thinking through whether a particular type of sponsorship, or even sponsoring a particular organization, is still relevant.

The way to try to identify sponsorships being selected on the basis of emotional issues is to ask for a robust business case. Most of these sponsorships will fail if an attempt is made to construct a viable business case as this should identify how the opportunity in question will under-perform in terms of achieving brand and business objectives.

Errors of judgement

Even when a robust selection process has been conducted, it is still possible to make genuine errors of judgement based on:

1. *Decisions made under time pressure.* As previously discussed in this chapter, time can be a real enemy to the sponsorship selection process and therefore, if in doubt, it is recommended that a sponsorship should not be rushed through based on the rights-holder's timeframe. There is no evidence of companies that have gone out of business because they decided not to take up a sponsorship opportunity as the timing was too short. Take a step back and save the money to spend on an alternative property with a less aggressive timetable or possibly invest in the same property next year having allowed sufficient time for thorough research and negotiation.
2. *Poor links between the property's fan base and the organization's target audience.* Considering the level of customer insight that most sponsors are used to, rights-holders still fail to address the need to make available at least basic demographic data to potential sponsors. The only solution to this is for sponsors to pre-test the sponsorship via focus groups. Looked at more deeply, it may be that what appeared to be a potentially strong property has a weaker link with the sponsor's target audience than originally perceived. Carrying out research via focus groups that discuss the organization in the

context of the property will provide the necessary feedback on whether this is actually the right match. An added bonus may be insights into ways in which the sponsor might make itself more relevant, and therefore more credible and attractive, to fans through targeted leveraging activity.

3. *Sponsorship is inappropriate to the organization's current stage in the brand/company lifecycle.* A carefully crafted sponsorship strategy must directly support marketing and business strategy. Sponsorship is not always an appropriate tool but may be entered into erroneously, often as the result of an emotions-based decision as discussed above. This is a very quick way for an organization to lose money and focus on key business drivers.

4. *Sponsorship lacks clear objectives.* Poorly conceived sponsorships are often tasked with achieving a plethora of diverse and ill-formed objectives that results in fragmented leveraging and little progress being made. Focusing on two or three really clear objectives that have been determined in advance of the sponsorship selection decision will assist in reducing the risk of choosing the wrong sponsorship.

5. *The wrong package of benefits is chosen.* An extreme example of this could be securing a title sponsorship when the primary objective was to showcase a product which could have been adequately achieved with a supplier level sponsorship and some additional hospitality negotiated on top of the rights-holder's standard offering. The solution here is to look at the total cost to service against the value delivered and to adopt the bottom-up approach to identify essential assets.

Many companies, including Sony Ericsson with the WTA women's tennis tour and O2 with Arsenal Football Club, have seen that, while being a top-level sponsor was right for them initially, later on it became inappropriate and they renegotiated their rights packages accordingly. There is no shame in reducing investment levels in line with business needs.

Key take-outs

- Do you need more sponsorship?
- Develop sponsorship criteria in advance and select on this basis.

- Agree and implement an appropriate sponsorship process.
- Ask business units what assets would be critical to them from each property and do not forget employee benefits.
- Negotiate for what you need, do not buy merely what the rights-holder wants to sell.
- Get professional help in negotiating and finalizing contracts.

Summary

The most important consideration is whether more sponsorship is really necessary prior to embarking on a sponsorship selection process that should be based on predetermined criteria. In no circumstances rely on the emotions of the Chairman's wife to influence sponsorship selection decisions. Ask departments and divisions what sorts of assets would be most useful to them and then, once a property is selected, negotiate hard for the necessary benefits to achieve the organization's sponsorship objectives. If things go wrong, identify the cause so that an appropriate solution can be found.

CHAPTER 4

SPONSORSHIP IMPLEMENTATION

 **Overview**

This chapter looks at the key ingredients of successful sponsorship implementation and considers how to focus expenditure on what is really important in terms of achieving the sponsor's objectives. Case studies will demonstrate some insightful and creative partnership activation.

This chapter covers:

- The key ingredients of successful sponsorship activation.
- Stimulating creative thinking around leveraging sponsorship properties.
- Issues and how to overcome them, both internally and externally.

Sponsorship implementation

Sponsorship implementation, otherwise known as sponsorship leveraging, activation or exploitation, is where all the planning and preparation turns into activity that is aimed at achieving the sponsor's objectives among the sponsorship's key target audience(s). Referring back to the European Sponsorship Survey (Figure 2.1), the elements that reflect successful sponsorship activation are:

- Sponsors need to have respect from the consumers or the fans, i.e. the sponsor's presence and contribution to the activity is recognized as beneficial in some way. This may be partially gained by creative activation of the sponsorship.

- Internally, sponsors need to ensure that the sponsorship is integrated across the organization, with the right internal team and buy-in from senior management.

The key ingredients of successful sponsorship activation

Figure 4.1 highlights the five key ingredients that combine together to create a successful sponsorship activation programme.

1. Assets

Assets, both tangible and intangible, have been discussed in Chapter 1 (see Table 1.1). As a reminder, tangible assets are those, such as branding on boards, hospitality, acquiring specialist expertise and use of meeting facilities, to which a financial value may be ascribed in some way. Intangible assets, on the other hand, are ethereal and their value cannot be calculated in financial terms. Intangible assets would include the value of category exclusivity, the importance of being associated with a particular set of brand attributes as

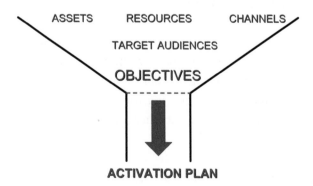

Figure 4.1 The key ingredients of successful sponsorship activation

espoused by the property or the networking opportunities presented by the property in terms of the other sponsors and stakeholders it attracts.

Clearly, not all available assets will be relevant to all sponsors' objectives. Therefore it is important for a sponsor to consider the extent to which each available asset is germane and how it might fit into their bespoke leveraging programme. While this is more obvious for tangible assets, it is also an important consideration for intangibles. For example, if category exclusivity is important, how will the sponsor ensure that the target audiences understand that the brand is an exclusive partner in a way that makes it more credible or important? If there are networking opportunities, which departments are best placed to make use of those opportunities and how will they be encouraged to get involved?

2. Resources

The number and type of resources that can be deployed in support of a sponsorship activation programme will determine the extent to which the assets can be leveraged. There are three main resource groups to take into consideration: financial, physical and human (people).

Financial

There is an industry norm which suggests that, for every $1 spent on the sponsorship fee, at least $1 should be spent on activation. While this is indicative, and a useful starting point for those new to investing in sponsorship, it is by no means written in stone. For example, where a sponsorship is primarily an efficient media buy, there may be little requirement to spend on activation beyond generating the most brand exposure that can be squeezed out of the property. Equally, many of the most successful sponsors will be investing considerably more than a ratio of 1:1, with one Olympic sponsor admitting to investing 7:1 on activation to rights in an Olympic year to optimize overall returns on their rights investment.

Where does all this money come from? Any successful sponsorship will require some budget to be set aside to support the basics of the sponsorship. These might include:

- employing a hospitality agency to manage the inventory and delivery of the organization's hospitality at the sponsored event.
- securing a photographic service to capture iconic moments and store these in an easy retrieval system.
- cross-funding the creation of content on the organization's intranet and website to communicate to both internal and external audiences around the sponsorship.

However, it is vital to remember that a successful sponsorship is one that is integrated across the organization and therefore this opens up other budgets in support. This is not about diverting money from anyone's budget towards the sponsorship team. Rather it is about each department identifying how best it can integrate the sponsorship into its own activities in pursuit of the sponsorship's objectives. For example:

- The marketing communications team was no doubt planning communications anyway; their challenge is to integrate the sponsorship into these in a meaningful way, whether that is advertising, public relations or sales promotions.
- The sales team will have a budget for entertaining prospects and clients; some of this may now be spent on purchasing sponsorship-related hospitality. Equally, the sales incentive programme may now incorporate rewards associated with the sponsorship.
- The corporate reputation team will be planning events to influence stakeholders; it may be that one or more of these events might be held at the rights-holder's venue.
- Human resources will have a budget to manage recruitment and employee retention; these could now incorporate imagery and other elements of the sponsorship to help the organization stand out from other employers.

There is also another budget in an organization, commonly know as the CEO's 'private pot'. In spite of all the effort invested in the annual planning process by large organizations, the Chief Executive nevertheless always seems to have some money squirreled away for discretionary spending. This is well worth remembering when a great activation opportunity surfaces that requires additional, tactical investment not accounted for elsewhere.

Physical

Physical resources often go under-utilized in activating a sponsorship. One of these could be available technology or providing simple materials, either raw, part-worked or ready for sale, to enhance your sponsorship activity and your relationship with your rights-holder. It may be that the organization is able to leverage its logistics operation to deliver promotional premiums or retail sites as a ticket distribution network. Brainstorming around the organization's core operations may produce some interesting and innovative opportunities that can be creatively woven into the sponsorship activation programme while also reducing costs.

People

People are really important in making a sponsorship happen, and the challenge for the sponsorship team is to draw on the range of human resources available both internally and externally. To be effective, the best people need to be brought in to bring their skills and knowledge to enhance the sponsorship project.

For example, who in the organization is a good creative thinker and could be persuaded to participate in a brainstorming session in the early days of planning the sponsorship to help to develop really good leveraging ideas? Who else might be skilled in implementation, administration, logistics, accounting, budgeting or managing hospitality? Who has strong formal and informal networks that can help to influence others and get things done? It might be possible to involve call centre staff in supporting the hospitality programme by taking reservations and understanding customers' individual needs.

Engaging these groups and individuals in the sponsorship in a way that helps them to understand what the sponsorship is all about for the organization will not only improve sponsorship outcomes but also help to overcome any internal resistance that can sometimes occur. This will be discussed in more detail later in this chapter.

3. Channels

Whilst currently channels like new media and social networks may be top of mind, an organization should interrogate itself thoroughly to identify as many

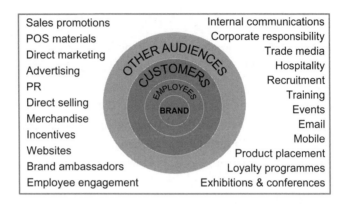

Sales promotions
POS materials
Direct marketing
Advertising
PR
Direct selling
Merchandise
Incentives
Websites
Brand ambassadors
Employee engagement

Internal communications
Corporate responsibility
Trade media
Hospitality
Recruitment
Training
Events
Email
Mobile
Product placement
Loyalty programmes
Exhibitions & conferences

OTHER AUDIENCES
CUSTOMERS
EMPLOYEES
BRAND

Figure 4.2 Possible channels to market

relevant channels as possible through which it might communicate the sponsorship. Figure 4.2 illustrates some of the possible channels to market that might be available. Examples of how some of these channels might be used include:

Advertising

Sponsorship-related advertising is a powerful method of amplifying a sponsorship's key messages. However, care should be taken not to promote different aspects of the brand to the sponsorship's target audience at the same time as the sponsorship to avoid customer confusion.

Incentives

These could be sales incentives or partner incentives for parts of the supply chain to encourage them to supply better, cheaper and/or higher quality products and services.

Other channels

It is important to remember that some channels may offer highly cost-effective routes to market. Some low cost or free channels include:

- *Internal:* email, intranet, magazines, canteen, notice boards, team meetings, reception areas.
- *Rights-holder:* advertising, ticket wallet, at event, magazine, audio-visual.
- *Indirect:* the media, fanzines.

4. Target audiences

As discussed in Chapter 1, sponsorship can target a wide range of audiences, but be quite clear that less is more. Do not have too many target audiences or, if that is impossible to avoid, prioritize two or three key target audiences and delegate lower priority audiences to the departments that normally manage these relationships. Any benefits gained via the sponsorship from these delegated audiences can be regarded as a bonus.

5. Objectives

Also discussed in Chapter 1, there are three different types of objectives for sponsorship: those that promote the brand, those that have unashamedly commercial outcomes, and those that are more around engagement, whether that is engaging employees, B2B customers or indeed a wider range of organizational stakeholders. A particular sponsorship's unique objectives form the mechanism through which the other "ingredients" will be filtered so that the sponsorship activation programme focuses on what is really important to the business. Being very clear about the two or three key objectives the sponsorship is aimed at achieving is highly beneficial in refining how resources will be allocated.

Integration

As highlighted in Figure 4.2, central to effective sponsorship integration is the organization's brand. Significant thought should be given to how the brand will be presented and therefore perceived within the context of the sponsorship.

The next most important issue to consider is employees and how to educate and engage them around the sponsorship. After all, if they do not understand why the organization is investing in this sponsorship and why it is relevant, how are they meant to talk about it effectively with the organization's stakeholders? This applies particularly to those who are customer facing, whether business-to-business or consumer.

This naturally leads to thinking about how this sponsorship is going to be relevant to customers or other target groups beyond them.

Developing a common understanding

It is important, particularly in a new sponsorship environment, for the sponsor's personnel to immerse themselves in the world of the rights-holder to develop a common understanding and aid communication. Equally, it is incumbent on the sponsor to educate the rights-holder's team about the organizatiion and what it is trying to achieve through the sponsorship. Key areas to focus on are highlighted in Table 4.1.

Table 4.1 Building shared understanding

The sponsored activity	The business arrangement
Scope	Partnership objectives
Rules	Contractual obligations
Vocabulary	Company jargon
Key players	Organization structures
Industry standards	Key contacts

Clearly, developing a deep understanding of each other's businesses and the challenges they present is not going to be achieved overnight. Research may be required to round out the picture, with further information potentially being available from:

- co-sponsors
- other clients
- governing bodies
- industry associations
- suppliers of related services

- case studies
- relevant business reports
- media coverage

Preparing for competitor response

The other issue that cannot be avoided is preparing for how competitors might respond to the organization announcing a new sponsorship. While the organization may feel very positive when the announcement is made, the possibility that competitors may take some action against it cannot be ignored (Figure 4.3).

Competitors may undertake a number of activities to reduce the positive impact of the sponsor's new project and undermine the organization's revenues. These may inevitably influence the sponsoring organization's corporate emotions and, to avoid this, it is essential to think through these particular scenarios and others that may be relevant to the business. Consider what competitors might do and how the organization can protect itself.

For example, if there is a likelihood that a competitor might ambush the sponsored activity, the organization should brainstorm all the ways that this

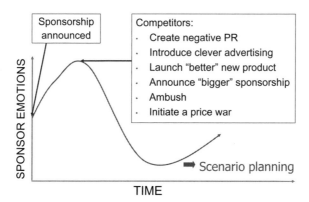

Figure 4.3 Possible competitor responses

could possibly be done, and put protections in place to ameliorate the worst effects. This should involve working closely with the rights-holder to close off certain possibilities that might occur within their sphere of influence.

Execution planning tips

While the main opportunities to secure sponsorship success have already been discussed, there are a few final issues that organizations need to take into account when implementing a new sponsorship programme.

Organizational lead times

If normal organizational lead times are long, perhaps associated with annual planning horizons, then that needs to be taken into account when implementing a sponsorship. Sponsorships have been likened to having babies: they come whether you are ready or not. One cannot postpone a birth any more than a rights-holder can postpone an activity just because a sponsor is not fully prepared. There is therefore a considerable responsibility resting on the sponsor to be ready to leverage the sponsorship in a timely manner and to have factored this issue into its planning across the organization.

Prioritize against anticipated value delivered

When comparing possible leverage activities, those that deliver better overall returns should be prioritized over those that may be more obvious but have less real payback. Preference must be given even if the particular idea will be harder to accomplish successfully.

Department by department

As mentioned in Chapter 3, plan department by department and ask colleagues, prior to contract, what they want in terms of assets and benefits that would be most useful to them. Once these assets are secured in the contract, these departments are now much more likely to use them and engage with the sponsorship, reducing the incidence of "not invented here" syndrome.

Ringfence activation budgets

This is very easy to say and very hard to get organizations to do. Activating the sponsorship is vital and people must realize that the sponsorship fee is only part of the investment. Not having a secure budget to activate a sponsorship is like paying the rental on a shop, but not stocking the store or dressing the window to attract customers inside. To achieve particular business and marketing objectives the activation budget is part of the total investment, it's not some sort of arbitrary add-on.

In crisis years, activation budgets have been one of the first places that large corporations have cut to reduce costs, which demonstrates a total lack of understanding of how sponsorship works. It is imperative that all sponsorship managers think about how to increase understanding of sponsorship within their organizations. It is critical that there is broad appreciation that protecting leveraging budgets is not a personal empire-building activity, but a necessity to protect the organization's investment in sponsorship in order to get an acceptable return for shareholders.

Agency alignment

It is very important to build trust and mutual support among any agencies supporting the sponsorship, such as an advertising agency, a PR agency, hospitality provider, or indeed a sponsorship consultancy. This can be a challenge but the best outcomes will only be achieved when everyone contributes and acts as seamless team members.

Internal communications for buy-in at all levels

Regular communications are critical to gaining support and buy-in at all levels across the organization for the sponsorship. Robust and repeated internal messaging not only ensures that colleagues are able to articulate the rationale for the sponsorship effectively, but there is also then less likelihood of the leveraging budget being pillaged when trading conditions deteriorate.

Human resources

A variety of human resources may be needed during the lifetime of a sponsorship, but not necessarily at the same intensity for the full period. Therefore, when and how to increase staff, as well as how to retrench effectively in quiet periods or as the sponsorship comes to the end of its life, needs to be given careful thought.

Execute creatively

Audiences are not waiting for the brand message. Activation must therefore reach out to the audience and be sufficiently engaging for them to notice the brand's presence and take in the key messages the sponsorship is aiming to communicate.

Message appropriately

Think through when and how consumers will encounter the brand in the context of the sponsorship, and understand what mood they might be in when that contact occurs. Either pick moments when they are likely to be receptive – for example, at half time when they are waiting for the action to restart – or tailor the message to fit in with their lack of receptiveness and use the media that is appropriate to each occasion.

Sponsorship is too often associated with being "just advertising" and consequently risks being treated with the same lack of engagement. For example, sponsors' digital perimeter display boards can be extremely distracting and intrusive to the on-pitch action. A sponsor's perimeter board will have much more impact if backed up by a message around the brand, showing what the sport means to the organization, why they are present, what they have contributed of value and therefore why the audience should think about buying the sponsor's products or services.

Case Study: Electronic gaming brand

 Key learning points:

- Brands are increasingly looking at new, non-traditional opportunities to engage with their target audiences.
- Direct engagement through sampling and experiential activity is becoming a more prominent element in the sponsorship mix.

An electronic gaming brand bought the rights to let the company activate in and around Twickenham Stadium during the Investec Challenge Series matches, The Nomura Varsity Match, The RBS Six Nations, The Emirates Airline London Sevens and the England versus Barbarians match. A spokesman for the brand explained the rationale by saying that "working alongside the RFU is a great opportunity for us to target and talk to a family audience, not just through traditional advertising methods but through a more experiential, hands on approach through product sampling."

Activation is a sensory experience

All aspects of the brand need to be considered in order to establish the most impactful ways to engage the target audience (see Figure 4.4). There may be strong visual aspects of the brand that can be leveraged in the sponsorship environment, or sounds might resonate. For some brands it may be smells, taste and touch that evoke the strongest response.

A friend is a Chelsea supporter and just the smell of the beer which is served at Chelsea immediately takes him back to being on the terraces. This shows the very strong relationship between a particular beer, its taste and smell, and a favourite sporting occasion.

How can the target audience touch the organization's brand in some similar way? The experiential element of sponsorship is becoming so much more important in allowing consumers to really engage with brands and become more deeply involved in how brands deliver authentic customer benefits.

Figure 4.4 Activate to appeal to the five senses

To provide some stimulus for brainstorming around sponsorship activation, Figures 4.5 to 4.7 suggest just some of the ways in which sponsorships might be brought alive to the key target audiences of employees (Figure 4.5), business-to-business (Figure 4.6) and consumers (Figure 4.7).

Figure 4.5 Reaching employees

Figure 4.6 Engaging B2B audiences

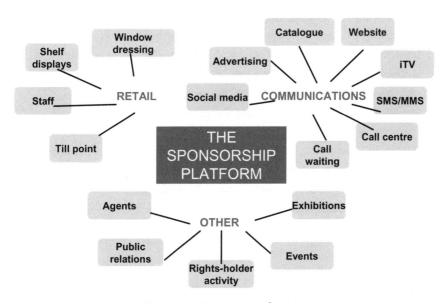

Figure 4.7 Consumer touchpoints

Below are three case studies of sponsorships targeting different audiences with an excellent degree of creativity and integration.

Case Study: The O2

Key learning points:

- Differentiation is one of the key attributes of a good sponsorship – sometimes a company needs a lot of courage to do something different.
- Imaginative use of the brand can provide subliminal cues that support more overt sponsorship leveraging.

It would be very difficult to talk about sponsorship implementation best practice without discussing O2 and how they have engaged with entertainment venues to really drive their brand forward.

O2 was facing the challenge of mobiles and networks becoming very commoditized. In an attempt to differentiate, competitors had introduced a variety of tariffs, but these only resulted in increased customer confusion over the best network for their needs. In addition, O2 operates in an industry where there is rapid convergence of mobile voice, video and data services which has intensified competition by introducing "non-traditional" players into the mobile market.

In order to really differentiate themselves O2 took the brave step of partnering with AEG, the venue operators of the former Millennium Dome in London. Apart from acquiring the title rights to the building, to bring the sponsorship alive, O2 integrated their branding into all aspects of the property, from using bubble-like shapes, blue lighting, blue carpets, and playing on the name of blue and O2 in the creation of indigo music club, O2 Blueroom Bar, O2 Lounge, and even O2 Angels in the Create zone.

But this sponsorship is more than merely brand association with music and entertainment. O2 also negotiated to introduce exclusive access for its customers. This includes priority ticket booking 48 hours in advance of public sale, bar and lounge access via mobile barcodes,

continued on next page ...

live music downloads, competitions, texting for tickets, changing wall-papers in the O2 Lounge, juke box requests and MMS of Create zone performances.

Outcomes were measured against core business objectives, with more than one million O2 customers signed for priority ticketing and over 200,000 for live music downloads and competition entries. Perhaps more importantly, there was a noticeably positive consideration differential (the closest predictor of market share) between those aware versus those unaware of The O2 sponsorship.

Such was the success of the O2 relationship, O2 have since expanded their reach by negotiating to include the Academy Music venues in the UK, the Sazka Arena in Prague and developing O2 World in Berlin and The O2 in Dublin.

(Reproduced with permission of O2)

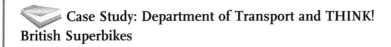 **Case Study: Department of Transport and THINK! British Superbikes**

 Key learning points:

- Sponsorship is not only useful to generate commercial returns (ROI) but can also successfully address other objectives (ROO), in this case behavioural change.
- Being sensitive to the target audience and giving them something they value is critical to being perceived as a valuable and credible partner by the audience.

Motorbike riders in the UK are predominantly male and are over-represented in road accident statistics. The British Department of Transport (DoT) wanted to reduce the number of accidents involving motorbikes but faced a challenge as to how to reach this group effectively. Rather than use advertising, which would both be expensive and

continued on next page ...

likely to be perceived as preaching and therefore ignored, the DoT invested in sponsoring the British Superbike Championship (BSB) which it has done since 2004.

British Superbikes attract a huge biker crowd, heavily indexed in favour of the DoT's target audience, with racing spread nationally across the summer season giving extensive coverage. The DoT used all the assets they could to leverage the appeal of the event and the star riders to connect with, rather than preach to, their elusive target audience. These included trackside branding using the already well-recognized yellow and black THINK! traffic safety campaign branding, a THINK! Motorcycle Academy trailer with interviews and signings from BSB stars, riding tips and advice from the Bikesafe Team, motorbikes on display, live BSB footage on plasma screens, interactive web stations and VIP Hospitality passes to be won every weekend.

There were measurable results, evaluation in 2009 showed that:

- 99% of respondents agree that "the THINK! campaign is a welcome sponsor of BSB";
- 95% agree that "the THINK! campaign is part of the biking community";
- 90% agree that "the THINK! campaign is relevant to me".

Source: TNS/DoT

Motorcycle fatalities fell by 16% in 2008, from 588 deaths in 2007 to 493 in 2008, and serious injuries by 10% from 6,149 to 5,556. This is an overall reduction in the rate of casualties of 2% (because motorcycle traffic fell by 8% over the period).

This sponsorship was not about selling anything, but about saving lives. What is interesting is that the research showed that BSB attendees actually welcomed what was, after all, government involvement, because they perceived that they actually got something relevant out of it for themselves.

(Reproduced by permission of Department of Transport)

Case Study: Spatone and athlete Lisa Dobriskey

Key learning points:

- A small budget should not be perceived as a barrier to sponsorship, merely a catalyst for greater creativity in activation.
- Other sponsors should not be perceived as competitors – rather explore what additional leveraging opportunities they might present.

Spatone, an iron-enhanced spring water product, needed to highlight the key messages of the brand as a solution to the symptoms of low iron levels in women. They affiliated with Lisa Dobriskey, Commonwealth champion at 1500 metres in 2006, and leading up to the 2012 London Olympics, and leveraged her other sponsor, Nike's, media interviews as an opportunity to mention Spatone.

Spatone became the UK's leading iron supplement and fastest growing brand in the iron supplement category in 2008-9. Spatone had a small budget but managed to develop a whole PR campaign around Lisa Dobriskey. They achieved excellent media coverage in mainstream media which translated into a direct impact on sales and market share of Spatone.

[Reproduced with permission of Spatone]

Implementation challenges and solutions

Co-ordination

A well-integrated sponsorship will, of necessity, need co-ordination across the organization to reduce the risk of duplication, incoherence, frustration and disengagement. While this applies at the departmental level, working across divisions and involving external parties such as agencies, suppliers and other business partners creates an additional layer of co-ordination complexity.

The only way to co-ordinate effectively is by regular and frequent communication, planning and engagement.

Ownership

Sponsorship is often perceived as being owned by the entire organization, but this can result in a lack of accountability for success. It is therefore very important when taking on a new sponsorship to be quite clear about who is going to be responsible for success, and to make sure that the other players understand their role and know who is ultimately in charge.

Budgeting

Sponsorship, unless carefully managed, can easily over-run on budget. In addition, an enormous amount of time can be wasted on internal charging, recharging, dealing with disputed charging and indeed, departments, divisions and external parties not paying. Make sure from the start that the accounting team supporting the sponsorship is first class, and that money moves around the organization with a minimum of administrative burden.

Cultural challenges

To be effective, sponsorships need widespread commitment but there are several internal obstacles to face including:

- Dislike of change
- Personal irrelevance
- "Distance" from sponsorship
- Internal politics
- Cynicism
- Lack of organizational energy

It is vital not to underestimate the internal selling effort required to implement a sponsorship successfully. It is, therefore, imperative to concentrate on this early and especially to identify the disenfranchised quickly before they undermine the sponsorship effort too far. It may not be possible to turn them into evangelists but at least their negativity can be neutralized.

Management involvement

Management involvement is a big challenge and very much dictated by the level of personal interest in the sponsorship, which is governed by:

- Perceived importance of the sponsorship to the organization
- Profile of the sponsorship externally
- "Not invented here" syndrome
- Level of interest from customers/stakeholders.

A good number of clients confess outright that their historical sponsorship decisions have been based on the personal interests of senior management. The regard management has for sponsorship in general is also linked to how important they feel the sponsorship is for the organization, and how they perceive the sponsorship as being seen externally.

There have been sponsorships that have gained absolutely no buy-in from the Board until one of their key contacts outside the organization mentions that they have seen it. This then results in an upsurge of attention on every facet of the sponsorship programme. Sponsorship managers need to be alert for this occuring. They risk being sandwiched between no leadership in the first instance, followed by too much involvement in decision-making around minor details, which results in erroneous prioritization and weakened outcomes.

Customers' reactions

If market research or other data provides evidence to indicate that customers have not noticed the sponsorship, this suggests that the sponsorship is failing to provide sufficient brand exposure. If there is no further opportunity to extend branding associated with the sponsorship, then leveraging with above-the-line advertising or point-of-sales material to supplement the mutual association should be contemplated. PR may also help to bolster sponsorship communication and show why the partnership is relevant to customers.

Alternatively, it may be that customers appear to have a good level of sponsorship awareness but, at the attitudinal level, it has not changed their consideration or preference for your brand. This may be a good time to call in an expert to give an external view to suggest how value might be added to make the sponsorship more relevant.

If customers' actual behaviour has not changed as anticipated, perhaps this can be incentivized via, for example, the use of promotions, loyalty schemes or other customer response mechanisms to get closer to them. Ultimately, it may be necessary to face the fact that the sponsorship was selected in error, at which point the best course of action is to plan and execute as swift and as dignified an exit as possible.

Multiple markets

Many sponsorships are in fact national in footprint, but larger ones can span several countries. Multi-market activation must take account of differing:

- Market development levels
- Legal environments
- Cultural diversity
- Demographic development
- Politics
- Social stability

There are two main approaches to multi-market activation. Either a "one size fits all" method can be adopted, which is resource efficient but might produce a sub-optimal result, or a "multi-local" activation plan may be preferred. This should be more effective as it is tailored to each market's individual needs, but it is very resource intensive to implement.

Co-sponsors

In a multi-sponsor environment all sponsors are to some extent competing for the rights-holder's scarce resources. One of the challenges is to identify those sponsors who share similar goals and may support joint activation tactics that leverage those scarce resources exponentially. The other issue to be aware of is resisting the temptation to be diverted by another sponsor's activation programme which appears superficially attractive, but may not be relevant in pursing your organization's own objectives.

 ## Key take-outs

- Understand what assets and resources you have to play with.
- Identify the most relevant marketing activities for achieving clearly defined objectives.
- Take account of organizational lead times.
- Prioritize against anticipated value delivered.
- Ringfence exploitation budgets.
- Remember internal communications to gain buy-in at all levels.

Summary

The cornerstone of successful sponsorship is to focus on objectives and target audiences. Filtering every leveraging idea through a lens that reflects a single-minded pursuit of goals will increase the chances of their achievement and reduce the likelihood of unnecessary expenditure on interesting but irrelevant diversions.

CHAPTER 5

SPONSORSHIP EVALUATION

🌐 Overview

This chapter aims to increase understanding of the merit of a proper evaluation programme for a sponsorship, and a better appreciation both of the theory and the practice. The benefits of setting SMART objectives, measuring return on investment (ROI) versus return on objectives (ROO) and the range of measurement methodologies that might be used, are discussed, with case studies to illustrate evaluation in practice.

This chapter covers:

- Developing a measurement programme
- SMART objectives
- ROI v. ROO
- Measurement methodologies
- The role of market research
- Inputs, outputs and outcomes
- Valuing media exposure
- The wrong reasons for renewal

Evaluation programme planning

While the review phase naturally falls towards the end of the sponsorship cycle it is important to remember that robust evaluation actually starts in the

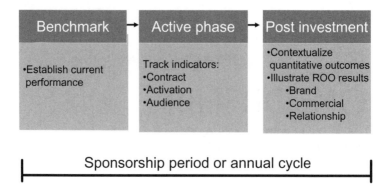

Figure 5.1 Evaluation programme plan

planning phase of a sponsorship (see Chapter 3). In order to measure sponsorship outcomes successfully it is essential that an evaluation blueprint for a sponsorship is created in advance of implementing the sponsorship. Results can then be tracked and, if necessary, adjustments made during the lifetime of the sponsorship to optimize returns.

A sponsorship evaluation programme has three phases, as highlighted in Figure 5.1.

The first stage reflects the importance of setting a benchmark, preferably before the activation programme is implemented and ideally before the sponsorship is even announced, so that the impact of the sponsorship on particular metrics can be clearly seen. That original definition of the status quo is the yardstick against which to assess results going forward. The challenge with establishing a benchmark is that often a sponsorship is already in place before evaluation is given much thought. Sponsorship managers may have inherited a sponsorship and are now expected to report on performance but find that no benchmark against which to judge success was ever recorded. The simple answer to this conundrum is to decide to create a benchmark now and measure progress going forward. This may not be a perfect solution but is wholly better than avoiding success measurement altogether.

The active phase of a sponsorship evaluation programme may involve tracking indicators, whether that is concerned with contractual compliance, sponsorship activation or how the audience is responding appropriately. If a sponsorship is contracted for a five-year period it may be acceptable to only review tracking data annually and use the information provided to change planned marketing activities for the following year to gain a greater level of engagement.

Some brands may have very good reasons why they measure more frequently, sometimes even more than once a month in the build up to a major event like the Olympics, for example. It all depends on the specific objectives and how closely performance must be monitored against those objectives in order to make sure that the desired outcomes are achieved.

For a sponsorship of a short-term festival or of only a few months' duration, it may be sufficient to simply establish a benchmark and then move straight to a post-investment review.

The third phase in a sponsorship evaluation programme is that which focuses on a post-investment review where a full understanding of performance from selected metrics will need to be reported. This may include how the brand has been developed, outcomes from commercial activities, or what relationships were built.

Use SMART objectives

A critical element of creating the evaluation blueprint is establishing SMART objectives for a sponsorship. SMART stands for:

- Specific
- Measurable
- Achievable
- Relevant
- Timebound

Setting SMART objectives is not easy and, as a result, many sponsorships are tasked with a plethora of vaguer objectives to make up for the fact that defining two or three SMART objectives was proving beyond the organization's capabilities and/or appetite for measurement. However, SMART objectives are critical to understanding the impact of a sponsorship investment.

Case Study: Multi-National Mobile Telecoms Brand

Key learning points:

- SMART objectives enable disciplined analysis of sponsorship performance.
- Measuring at this level makes it much easier to explain sponsorship returns and justify sponsorship investments.

Table 5.1 SMART objective for a team sponsorship

Objective	Increase unaided awareness of the sponsored Team (cycling) amongst 18-35 year old men in Germany from 5% to 15% by 31 December 2008.
Measurement methodology	Tracked via changes in sponsor's brand tracker responses in the German market using this month's data as the benchmark.
Frequency	Quarterly
Rationale	Brand awareness "primes the pump" for future sales.

The multi-national mobile telecoms network in the case study above set the SMART objective shown in Table 5.1 for their sponsorship of a specific sports team.

This is a SMART objective because it is:

Specific: Unaided awareness is specified, as opposed to aided awareness, as are the gender, age group and a particular geographic market.

Measurable: It is very measurable because it was tracked via changes in the quarterly brand tracker. The starting month was defined as the benchmark in advance of the sponsorship activity being implemented to enable an understanding of the shift in awareness from before the sponsorship appeared in-market. Another point in its favour, although not strictly related to setting SMART objectives, is that it uses a measurement tool already in place. This is cost-efficient because measuring this objective required little extra expense as the company simply had to add a question to their brand tracker rather than create a whole new market research study.

Achievable: Clearly the company at the time this objective was set felt that to lift awareness from 5% to 15% over the course of a 12 month period was an ambitious but manageable target.

Relevant: This objective was very relevant because, by increasing awareness of the sponsorship it helped to establish the foundation on which sales could be built in future. It made people more familiar with the brand name and associated the brand with a sport that was dynamic and fast, key attributes customers look for in a mobile network service.

Timebound: A very definite end date was set by which they wanted to have achieved this increase in unaided awareness, 31st December 2008.

Sponsorship impacts

There are three different types of sponsorship impact: inputs, outputs and outcomes (see Table 5.2). It is very important to understand the differences as best practice sponsorship evaluation focuses on measuring outcomes.

The amount of media coverage that is generated by a sponsorship, or the estimated value of that media coverage, is an input. It means little as a piece of data in itself apart, perhaps, from the ability to compare visibility year on year. It does not reveal whether anybody actually noticed the sponsorship, or

Table 5.2 **Sponsorship inputs, outputs and outcomes**

	Sponsorship impacts
Inputs	Amount of media coverage
	On-site exposure
	Likely audience exposed to property advertising
	Branded marketing materials produced and circulated
	Number of attendees
Outputs	Changes in attitudes to the brand
	Numbers signing up to a loyalty programme
	Improved B2B relationships
Outcomes	Improvements in customer purchase frequency and/or loyalty
	Sales achieved
	Commercial impacts of improved B2B relationships

if it changed the way they thought, or their behaviour. Therefore, unless the main objective of the sponsorship is an efficient media buy, as outlined in the Vodafone case study in Chapter 1, think carefully before spending a significant proportion of the evaluation budget on media evaluation.

It is the same with on-site branding; one hundred thousand people may have walked past on-site branding but did anybody actually notice it? Did it change their opinion, or did it change their actions with regard to the sponsor's brand as a result?

The benefit of input measures is that they are relatively easy to quantify and media evaluation, particularly, tends to exhibit a reassuringly positive number that can be put in front of the Board showing a "profit" of equivalent media value returned against the rights fee paid. However, the disadvantage is that there is no way to tell whether the brand exposure actually made any difference. Therefore, while there is no reason not to collect input measures, it is necessary to understand their relatively low value in terms of their contribution to an overall sponsorship evaluation.

Sponsorship outputs

Outputs are definitely an improvement on inputs as they measure changes in the target audience's attitudes to the brand as a result of being exposed to a sponsorship. Attitude shifts are normally measured by market research, or perhaps by the numbers of people signing up to the brand's loyalty programme if an element of sponsorship activation included a promotion to increase the number of loyalty programme members. Improved business-to-business relationships would also certainly count as an output.

Sponsorship outcomes

The Holy Grail of sponsorship evaluation is calculating the real outcomes from a sponsorship. Sponsorship outcomes demonstrate the reality of a sponsorship's performance.

The figure that most senior managers would like to have reported is the link between sales and sponsorship activity. This is difficult because it is hard to isolate sponsorships from the other elements of the marketing mix; there are external events, competitor activity, even seasonal variations that affect sales. Some tracking can nevertheless be done through promotional coupons, purchase frequency or business-to-business benefits, for example. While it is accepted that this measure is a challenge, sponsorship managers should still actively pursue data relating to this outcome if a direct sales impact was a key objective of the sponsorship.

ROI v. ROO

Historically there has been a lot of focus on measuring Return on Investment (ROI), a financial metric. ROI is the gain from an investment minus the cost of that investment, divided by the cost of that investment and mathematically it is expressed by the following equation:

$$ROI = (Gain\ from\ investment - Cost\ of\ investment)\ /\ Cost\ of\ investment$$

To give an example, imagine a small sponsorship with total costs including fees and activation of \$80,000 but a total value created calculated at \$125,000:

$$ROI = (\$125,000 - \$80,000)\ /\ \$80,000 = 0.562$$

The return on investment is 0.562. To be more meaningful, most people tend to think of return on investment in percentage terms and most companies have a hurdle rate return on investment against which they measure potential performance. To convert ROI to a percentage, the following equation is used:

$$ROI = (\$125,000\ /\ \$80,000) \times 100 = 156.25\%$$

This is normally represented as a return on investment of 56.25%, that is, the original investment has been recouped in full, plus a further 56.25% of incremental profit has been delivered by the original investment of \$80,000.

Applying ROI as a measurement methodology is attractive because it is a commonly used method for measuring business returns and this, therefore (in theory), allows comparisons between investments in sponsorship versus other options. Indeed, much effort has been expended trying to create a methodology that will enable ROI for all sponsorships to be calculated and direct comparisons made.

Table 5.3 ROI v. ROO

ROI	ROO
Cash based	Variety of "currencies"
Values outcomes in terms of financial efficiency	Values outcomes in terms of how well objectives have been achieved

The issue with this approach is that it fails to take into consideration the multiplicity of objectives that any single sponsorship might be tasked with achieving, many of which do not have direct financial returns, such as the THINK! British Superbikes campaign outlined in Chapter 4. Therefore, when considering how to measure sponsorship, Return on Objectives (ROO) has now become the favoured approach.

The differences between ROI and ROO are highlighted in Table 5.3. As discussed, ROI is very much a cash-based financial value. It values outcomes in terms of their financial efficiency: how much money was spent and how much was returned from that outlay? In theory it should be possible to look at different sponsorships, or indeed different aspects of the marketing mix, and identify which was the most efficient in terms of finance expended versus value gained from that expenditure.

The first difference with ROO is that it has a variety of 'currencies'. Of course, it is possible to have "achieving a particular return on investment" as one objective of a sponsorship, in which case the 'currency' would be cash based. However, other currencies could include increased percentage points of brand awareness or the numbers of people that have been entertained in sponsorship-related hospitality. Indeed, in the THINK! British Superbikes case (see Chapter 4) the 'currency' is lives saved.

The second difference between ROI and ROO is that ROO values outcomes in terms of how well the objectives have been achieved. There is at least one professional services firm where the sponsorship programme has no specific return on investment objectives. The firm's objectives are about relationship building and so their measurements in terms of achieving those objectives, and therefore their returns, are focused on how many relationships they have built, the manner in which they were built, and their relative strength, using the sponsorship programme as a platform. They even have a score for how people inside the organization rate each relationship on a scale of 1 to 5. The effectiveness of the sponsorship is therefore calculated on how strongly it has contributed to increasing these relationship measurement metrics. The firm does not value their returns in cash at all. In fact, in cash terms they see investment in sponsorship as the equivalent of a retailer's 'loss leader' – as money spent to attract people in rather than make a direct contribution to the bottom line.

Measurement methodologies

There are essentially three types of measurement methodology from which sponsorship evaluation metrics can be created, as illustrated in Table 5.4.

When discussing sponsorship measurement and evaluation, most people immediately think of market research. This has an important role in sponsorship evaluation and can be used at all stages of the sponsorship cycle to contribute insight and understanding (see Figure 5.2). First, market research can assist brands in considering what their real brand attributes are, the sorts of brand attributes they would like to associate with, and what their market priorities might be. In selection terms, market research will help to ascertain the property or properties that best fit with the audience perceptions, both for the brand as it is perceived today and how it might be developed in the future. During the sponsorship implementation phase, market research can be used to look at the effect of a sponsorship versus other activities in the marketing mix. Certainly in the review phase, market

Table 5.4 Sponsorship measurement methodologies

Quantitative	Qualitative	Other
SMART objectives rely on quantitative data to provide robust results: • Target audience demographics • Attitudes • Interests • Brand perceptions, usage & attitudes	Provides context and/ or deeper insights than quantitative research: • Focus groups • Interviews	All other sources of data: • Sales results • Market share • Employee turnover • Share price

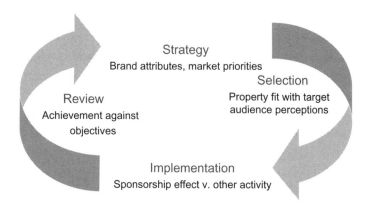

Strategy
Brand attributes, market priorities

Selection
Property fit with target
audience perceptions

Review
Achievement against
objectives

Implementation
Sponsorship effect v. other activity

Figure 5.2 The role of market research

research can be very useful in evaluating achievement on some types of objectives.

Quantitative research

Quantitative research involves gathering data from a statistically significant number of respondents from which conclusions can be drawn as to the overall impact on the whole target audience. This can be done face to face, or by postal or email questionnaire. However, the internet has made all research cheaper, and sports fans especially are one of the few groups keen to give their opinions for free. Online surveys have reduced the time needed to collect survey data and significantly reduced the costs of research, thus making it affordable even for smaller sponsorships. Although the sample is perhaps not always perfectly representative, online surveys can generate a wealth of actionable information for the sponsor.

Qualitative research

Qualitative research tries to understand the drivers of behaviours by using a relatively small number of respondents but a much deeper probe into sponsorship effects. Whereas quantitative research looks at large numbers of people answering fairly straightforward multiple-choice questionnaires, qualitative focus groups and interviews provide greater contextual detail. The disadvantage of qualitative research is that it is very expensive and therefore is usually used only for high-value sponsorships.

Other measurement methodologies

Market research is an obvious way of understanding how a sponsorship is progressing, but is by no means the only methodology available for measuring sponsorship outcomes. Other data can be a rich source of feedback. While undertaking a project on behalf of the European Sponsorship Association, other sources of data were identified for approximately 40 different possible sponsorship objectives.

One example is demonstrated in Table 5.5, which illustrates the variety of measurement methodologies that might be deployed to evaluate success against an objective of building brand loyalty. The (very measurable) objective of this sponsorship was that the customer purchased the sponsoring brand to fulfil at least 60% of their total needs for this product or service.

For illustrative purposes, assume that this is shampoo brand X and that, even if different family members use different shampoos, 60% of the total

Table 5.5 Example measurement methodologies for the objective of building brand loyalty

Objective	Qual.	Quant.	Other	
Increase or maintain customer loyalty to brand – customer to purchase brand to fulfil 60% or more of total need for this product or service	√ √			• Quantitative research to ascertain claimed purchase levels, comparing those exposed and not exposed to sponsorship. • Qualitative research to contextualize differing levels of loyalty between exposed/not exposed.
			√	• Loyalty programme purchase behaviour tracking
			√	• Share of wallet tracking via purchase panel membership
			√	• Retention rates on contract renewal between exposed/not exposed

household shampoo spend is made up of that brand. The options for how one might ascertain success are listed on the right-hand side of the chart and qualified as a quantitative, qualitative or other technique in the middle columns.

The straightforward way is to ask a representative sample of people via market research such questions about brand X as:

- *Are you buying this shampoo?*
- *Which other shampoos do you buy, if any?*
- *How many people are there in your household?*
- *How many of them use this shampoo?*
- *Do any of them use other similar products that they purchase themselves?*
- *Of all of the shampoo consumed in your household, what percentage would you say is this shampoo?*
- *Are you aware of any sponsorship undertaken recently by this shampoo?*
- *If yes, what sponsorship(s) have you heard about?*

The answers are then tabulated and checked, especially as to respondents claimed purchase levels. The classic technique in sponsorship research is to compare those who are aware of a specific sponsorship promoting the brand X shampoo with those not aware of the sponsorship. Any resulting differences in product purchasing habits, all other things being equal, suggest the degree to which the sponsorship is enticing more people buy brand X shampoo, and whether or not these customers are sufficiently 'loyal' to brand X shampoo as defined in the objective.

Qualitatively one could then probe more deeply and look at the two different groups – exposed and not exposed – as to what is really driving their purchase decision. This would help to understand what elements of the sponsorship have been the key drivers of brand X loyalty, and whether there are other leveraging opportunities that might influence a wider group of those exposed to be even more loyal to the brand.

Another legitimate way of tracking in this example could be the use of loyalty programme data from the major supermarket chains to understand exactly which customers are actually purchasing the product, and indeed purchasing competitors' products. Over time, this is likely to give a more accurate indicator of the real sales differential than claimed purchase habits, especially if several sponsorship-related promotions are run in one chain or area, with another chain or area acting as the control group.

In some industry sectors and markets there is something called a purchase panel, which is where a cross-section of people provide their sales receipts on a weekly basis to an organization which then encodes them. This provides an understanding of everything that that household has spent, and this method should provide the most robust data into actual purchase behaviours for this particular product.

Finally, if this was not a shampoo but some sort of subscription product such as a magazine, another example could be retention rates on contract renewal between those exposed and those not exposed. This measure can be applied in both consumer and business-to-business environments.

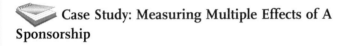 **Case Study: Measuring Multiple Effects of A Sponsorship**

 Key learning points:

- There are a variety of tools that can be used to qualify sponsorship performance.
- Do not be afraid to test tools to see which ones work best in particular situations.

When the European zonal management of a global retail brand found itself required to provide input into whether the its major global sponsorship platform should be renewed, it realized that no SMART objectives had been recorded at the beginning of the sponsorship term and there was little data on which to base an opinion. In addition, there were many polarized emotions within the organization; people either loved the sponsorship, and could see a plethora of benefits being accrued by

continued on next page ...

the business from the sponsorship investment, or they thought it was a total waste of money and wanted absolutely nothing to do with it.

Eventually the zone made the recommendation that the best action was to renew the sponsorship for another five years. This was based on the fact that no evidence could be found that suggested that the sponsorship was doing the brand or business any harm. Some data also seemed to point to the possibility that the sponsorship had made a positive impact.

However, zonal management was determined that it would not find itself in the same position when the contract came up for its next renewal. Future renewals would be decided using data and a three phase action plan was put in place to make this a reality. First, it was important to have more and better data at the macro level. Second, in order to measure some specific projects and see how those might act as proxies for other projects being promoted, further micro level data was required. Finally, there was a new focus on making this data available and ensuring that senior management was aware of the results so that they understood how this sponsorship was actually delivering for their business.

Phase 1: Macro level data expansion
The first action was to look at the global brand tracker and the questions that were being asked that were related to the sponsorship (see Figure 5.3).

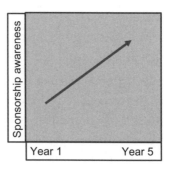

Figure 5.3 Global brand tracker results

continued on next page ...

To increase the robustness of the data in key markets the brand:

- doubled its sample sizes.
- insisted that all markets tracked the sponsorship-related questions every year to provide a clearer picture of performance.

Once the data was being reported, the zone was able to demonstrate that sponsorship awareness among the target audience increased substantially.

However, this was top line data and therefore the brand wanted to understand better what was going on in key markets that were felt to be representative of the overall business across Europe.

Phase 2: Micro level detail enhancement
The brand recognized that the strength of the sponsorship relationship and how it was leveraged differed substantially across Europe and wanted to better understand these differences and the impacts they had on the overall results. It therefore initiated a number of projects that were tasked with providing more insight into these issues.

Sponsorship performance research
The brand instigated market research into sponsorship performance in a number of key markets that represented different facets of the sponsorship relationship. The objectives of the research were to:

- Measure sponsorship performance v. objectives
- Identify strengths and weaknesses
- Draw conclusions and make actionable recommendations
- Determine year on year performance

continued on next page ...

A research company assisted in tracking the results and the differences between markets provided essential data as to how the sponsorship worked in different market environments (see Figure 5.4).

Media exposure measurement
One of the arguments that had been put forward for not renewing the sponsorship was that brand exposure through sponsorship did not compare well with advertising (see Figure 5.5). Having renewed the sponsorship for a further term, a specialist exposure monitoring agency was hired to supply data to inform the debate.

While the brand recognized that media exposure valuation was a weak metric, tracking the value, and applying a discount rate to recognize the difference between advertising and sponsorship exposure, demonstrated that the sponsorship did have a role, especially in those markets where little or no television advertising was being funded.

Network sales
While accepting that the sponsorship-related sales network was smaller than those of some other marques, sales via this channel still represented

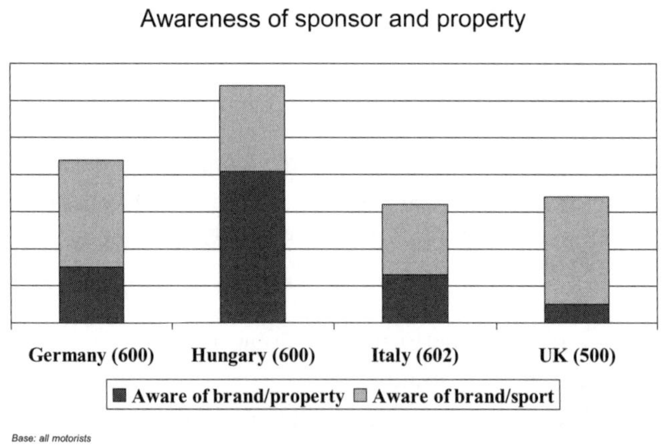

Awareness of sponsor and property

Germany (600)   Hungary (600)   Italy (602)   UK (500)

■ Aware of brand/property   ☐ Aware of brand/sport

Base: all motorists

Figure 5.4 Sponsorship tracker results

continued on next page …

a direct return on the sponsorship investment. The brand therefore started tracking sales through this channel including both direct sales to the rights-holder and those through the rights-holder's after sales network (see Figure 5.6).

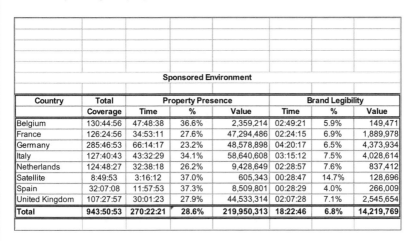

Country	Total	Property Presence			Brand Legibility		
	Coverage	Time	%	Value	Time	%	Value
Belgium	130:44:56	47:48:38	36.6%	2,359,214	02:49:21	5.9%	149,471
France	126:24:56	34:53:11	27.6%	47,294,486	02:24:15	6.9%	1,889,978
Germany	285:46:53	66:14:17	23.2%	48,578,898	04:20:17	6.5%	4,373,934
Italy	127:40:43	43:32:29	34.1%	58,640,608	03:15:12	7.5%	4,028,614
Netherlands	124:48:27	32:38:18	26.2%	9,428,649	02:28:57	7.6%	837,412
Satellite	8:49:53	3:16:12	37.0%	605,343	00:28:47	14.7%	128,696
Spain	32:07:08	11:57:53	37.3%	8,509,801	00:28:29	4.0%	266,009
United Kingdom	107:27:57	30:01:23	27.9%	44,533,314	02:07:28	7.1%	2,545,654
Total	943:50:53	270:22:21	28.6%	219,950,313	18:22:46	6.8%	14,219,769

Figure 5.5 Media exposure valuation

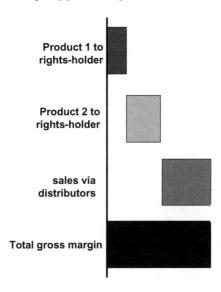

Figure 5.6 Network sales gross margin

continued on next page ...

The biggest contributor to margin was sales via distributors, which also carried a significantly higher gross margin and therefore contribution to the bottom line.

Merchandise

As part of the sponsorship, the brand was able to stock and sell the rights-holder's merchandise in the brand's network but historically this had been leveraged rather arbitrarily by market. Trials were therefore undertaken to better understand the role that selling this type of merchandise might play in the retail mix.

The conclusion was that different markets supported different types of proposition. Perhaps counter-intuitively, the brand found they could sell more, higher value, merchandise, and hence make significant sums from it, in less mature markets. In more mature markets the most effective merchandise operation was quite small, offering items like key rings. This research assisted in planning shop space to maximize profits on the whole range (see Figure 5.7).

Hospitality

Researching the impact of hospitality on guests was recognized as a challenge. At an event no guest wishes to be approached by someone

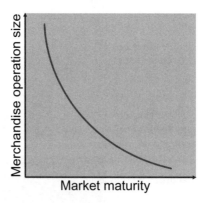

Figure 5.7 Merchandise research outcomes

continued on next page ...

with a clip-board asking them to rate their experience. However, one advantage of this sponsorship was the transfer times from the event by coach which provided an ideal opportunity for guests to complete a feedback questionnaire in their own time. This opportunity was used to gather useful data on both the hospitality experience and its stated impact on guests.

The survey suggested that there was a very positive shift in feeling more favourable to doing business with the brand among those people who were entertained (see Figure 5.8).

However, the brand recognized that people who have been the recipients of rather impressive hospitality will normally have a desire to be polite. Therefore they also tracked the sales resulting relating to the corporations of those people entertained. This established that, where representatives from a business had been entertained in a sponsorship-related environment, the annual gross

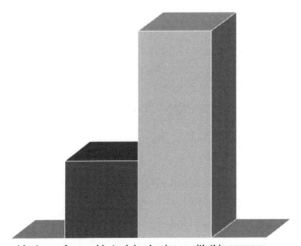

I feel more favourable to doing business with this company

■ **Year 1** ■ **Year 2**

Figure 5.8 Hospitality impact

continued on next page ...

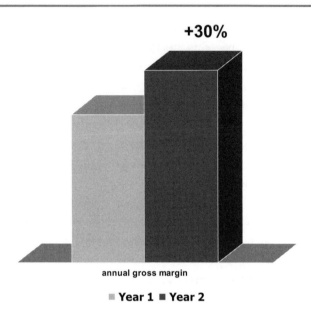

Year 1 ■ Year 2

Figure 5.9 Direct sales tracking

margin of sales to those businesses increased by 30% year on year compared to an 8% overall for the markets in which the businesses were located (see Figure 5.9). This suggested that sponsorship-related entertainment was not a waste of money but a serious business investment.

Internal best practice
One intriguing initiative was to evaluate the sponsorship through the introduction of an internal Sponsorship Awards. The main purpose of these internal awards was to capture and share impactful activation ideas across the decentralized, multi-market organization. Winners were reported in internal media with awards ceremonies conducted by a senior manager in each market.

continued on next page ...

The awards generated more than sixty data-based best practice case studies that were categorized and shared across all markets. This initiative was particularly clever as it cost virtually nothing to implement and reduced the amount of money spent on re-inventing the wheel on similar programmes across markets.

Phase 3: Regularized reporting

As well as the Sponsorship Awards, the European Board received an annual key performance indicator (KPI) report that covered both the brand measures and the business results that were being tracked.

In addition, a formal midterm review was held so that there was a clear understanding of what had been achieved to date and how far they intended to go before a re-signing decision was to take place. There is a saying 'what gets measured gets done', but also what gets reported gets prioritized, and regular reporting was essential in educating the European Board in advance of making their next renewal decision.

Positive outcomes

Overall the positive outcomes were that the brand was able to provide a robust, rational input to the next re-signing decision. The value derived from the sponsorship was clearly understood by senior management so they could all form rational opinions about the benefits it delivered to the bottom line.

The sponsorship had also been successfully repositioned from something that was considered irrelevant in some European markets to a much more European focused investment. It then became treated as such, and gained the appropriate level of attention from the Board as a result.

Having developed these methodologies around this sponsorship, the brand was then able to roll these out to other major sponsorships so developing their own best practice in evaluation as well as in activation.

The wrong reasons for renewal

A common problem faced by organizations, which results in their retaining a sponsorship long after its useful life, is the perception that if the organization drops a sponsorship, a competitor will step in to the detriment of the organization's business. The solution to this is similar to potential competitor behaviour on signing a new sponsorship, namely scenario planning. In some sectors where there are few competitors, modelling potential competitor response is critical, such as carbonated soft drinks or credit cards. This may be a challenge but the evidence should be reviewed very thoroughly if that is the only reason for retaining a particular sponsorship.

Too often sponsorships continue for years because nobody has really paid any attention to renewal, and decision-making becomes automatically favourable because nobody seeks to challenge the status quo. The reason that this might happen is that the organization may not realize that their objectives have changed. In today's fast-moving marketing environment sponsorships can quickly become no longer fit for purpose. In order to counteract this, any sponsorship should be regularly reviewed against marketing strategy to make sure that the investment is continuing to deliver on the marketing objectives.

Another retention challenge arises through corporate emotional baggage. When an organization has invested in a sponsorship over a long period, and senior management have grown to enjoy it and know all the key players personally, it gets progressively harder for the organization to make a rational re-investment decision. If a sponsorship is no longer relevant, it becomes encumbent on the sponsorship manager to try to disprove retention arguments through hard data. Of course, senior management may chose to ignore or disbelieve the data, at which point it may be best to seek a new position where sponsorship is given appropriate respect.

Key take-outs

- Create your evaluation blueprint during the planning phase rather than leaving it too late and then not having the data required to track sponsorship performance, and especially inform a renewal decision.

- Set a benchmark, preferably before initiating a sponsorship, so that the impact of the sponsorship can be clearly articulated via relevant sponsorship metrics.
- SMART objectives are challenging to create but the effort expended will be repaid fully in simplifying results tracking.
- Remember that ROO has a variety of currencies.
- Market research is a valuable data-gathering tool, but is not the only one available to evaluate sponsorship outcomes.
- Don't put too much value on input measures in a sponsorship evaluation: outputs and outcomes are more valid measures.
- Try to get the balance right between understanding the impacts and the outcomes and do not overspend on evaluation for its own sake.
- Don't renew simply because of the fear that a competitor will take your place and leverage the sponsorship more effectively. Priorities change over time and best practice organizations rigorously review all sponsorships on a regular basis.

Summary

Data-based measurement and evaluation is a real challenge but essential to understanding sponsorship performance. Resist the temptation to avoid evaluation and use SMART objective setting as the cornerstone of an effective evaluation framework. As the saying goes, "Rome was not built in a day", and that similarly applies to an effective evaluation programme. It may take time and effort to create, but the results will prove the power of sponsorship as a credible marketing discipline.

Part II

Sponsorship Seekers

CHAPTER 6

DEVELOPING A SPONSORSHIP STRATEGY

Overview

This section of the book is designed specifically for sponsor seekers, who are known more usually in sponsorship as "rights-holders" or sometimes "sponsees".

We start by focusing on the thinking that should ideally go on at the very beginning of developing a sponsorship programme for your organization.

- We show how having a good strategy from the outset, or working harder on your existing strategy, really helps you to upgrade and improve when you get to the most important part of the chain – the sales process.
- The simple fact to remember is that your view of the offering may be very different from that of a sponsor. They will view your pride and joy – maybe an activity or an event in which you have invested hours and hours of time and much personal commitment – simply as a tool (often among many alternatives) with which to help them to achieve their own objectives.

In this chapter we explain that:

- Modern sponsorship is much more about creative marketing than just buying exposure.
- Your sponsorship may have to appeal to several departments inside the same company, especially when they are all sharing the payment of your fee from their own budgets.

- It is important to present material that details any prior experiences with sponsors you may have had, as these are gold dust in helping to convince sponsors that they will be well looked after.
- Reviewing and refreshing your assets is a vital step in setting the strategy that will help you to sell more successfully.
- Sponsors are ever more demanding, and your strategy must take account of the manpower, resources and budget you will need to service the sponsorship that will lead eventually to successful renewals.
- Bothering to create a strategy will also insure and protect you against internal changes in the future, such as new management that might question the rationale of a particular sponsorship.
- You can only really show the successful results you have achieved personally by measuring against benchmarks originally set out in a written sponsorship strategy.
- It is worth thinking about and formally recognizing the internal challenges you might face if sponsorship is brought into your organization. This includes the manpower needed to handle sponsors, tax liability, possible reduction of any public money you may receive, and worries about undue influence from sponsors. Using case studies we show that sponsors can bring you benefits just as valuable as cash, such as benefit or marketing in kind.
- We show how important it is to understand your values and image and how the outside world sees you; how to show sponsors the type of audience you can bring them; and how to incorporate best practice from competitors into your own offering.

What modern sponsors want

Sponsorship has now gone a long way beyond a few logos and boards, some hospitality tickets and an exchange of money. It is also not to be confused with philanthropy (and that is one reason why we hate seeing "Gold, Silver and Bronze" packages because that gives the idea that sponsorship is somehow similar to just giving to a good cause). It is now seen by companies as something much more sophisticated. We are moving from being viewed as a sort of sub-set of advertising that sold logos and exposure and cost per thousands and impressions, into a much more creative phase – which is actually good for everybody in sponsorship.

Sponsorship is becoming very much more mixed in with the other activities of a company, as the best companies are viewing sponsorship as part of building their brand – not an isolated activity in itself. Departments such as PR and marketing, direct sales, and CSR often have some say, and indeed are often asked to share the cost of the sponsorship. Therefore your eventual proposal must be able to appeal to more than one department in a company.

Sponsors are above all looking to create situations where they can get in touch with a group they want to reach in a positive memorable setting, often referred to as creating "consumer touch points". This means that the job of the rights-holder, when thinking about strategy, is to look for what assets you have to offer that a sponsor could not possibly purchase anywhere else, and assure them that you will be introducing them to a group of people on whom they want to make a good impression.

So, knowing all that, how do we fix our strategy so that we get it right from the outset? This is how the process of sponsorship would appear in an ideal world as seen in Figure 6.1, which is a step-by-step guide to thinking about a strategy from the sponsor seeker's point of view.

If strategy is very much the first point of departure, what kind of things should we be looking for at this stage?

Making an historical review of sponsorship in your organization

The first thing is to collect anything that has been done before and any prior experiences of sponsorship within the organization, as these are often under-valued. The experience of successfully handling a sponsor has an impact on future sponsors because it gives you a certain pedigree and assures the sponsor that they will be looked after.

We recommend that you:

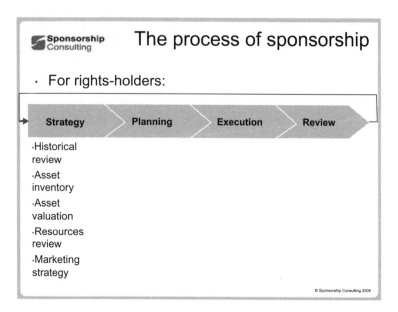

Figure 6.1 Step-by-step strategy guide

- Collect and list the names of any previous sponsors (or "near misses" that at one time were interested in becoming sponsors and may be again).
- See if any testimonials or references exist from that sponsor or, if practical, contact them and see if you can obtain one. (This can also be a prelude to eventually obtaining a repeat of the sponsorship.)

Asset inventory

If you are considering whether sponsorship is the appropriate thing to do, or if you are upgrading your current approach, you will be thinking about the assets in your cupboard that can be brought out and sold.

A full Asset Checklist Tool appears in Chapter 7 but Table 6.1 shows four very broad headings of sponsor's needs where sponsors look to see if you are bringing value.

After thinking about the areas in the table, a regular follow-on question is how to put a value on your package, but far too often this is done in terms of how much it costs you to run the activity, not how much value it represents to the sponsor. The next chapter will show you how to value the package.

Table 6.1 Checklist of needs

Sponsor needs	Action required
1. A useful connection to a target group	• Have you any existing information, and can you describe to sponsors what kind of people your fans or audiences are? • Be clear that you will be telling the sponsor that you know a lot about those people, and that they are attractive and will in some way be bringing a benefit to that sponsor. You are delivering connections, audiences of engaged people that the sponsor can meet and talk to almost in a one to one relationship. • Consider carrying out a survey now, (among event spectators for example) to collect some data that can be used later on in the sales process.
2. Exposure	• While sponsors today are perhaps more aware of the importance of leveraging and using a sponsorship to provide more than just exposure, the amount of exposure you can offer is still hard currency in the sponsorship world. Whether it's a small event in the local press, or if it is the FIFA World Cup with billions following it on television, millions of dollars of sponsorship per year gets traded on the back of it all around the world.
3. Image transfer	• In part, sponsors want the equity of your image brought to work for them. • Therefore being able to describe exactly what it is you represent and the values that you hold is important and most rights-holders need to work harder on this when they think about sponsorship. • Work on defining or redefining your core values and image attributes so that a sponsor will be able to fully understand the value you bring.

Resources review

When it comes to the resources you have behind your sponsorship efforts, it is very important to remember that sponsorship is incredibly consuming of manpower. This is true for the sponsor, and also for you the rights-holder because having sponsors means continual servicing and a lot of care to react to changing situations and demands. There will be an impact on costs and personnel, and this is something to be considered very carefully inside the organization.

Sponsorship strategy

The result of all this should be the formation of a clear statement of what has to be achieved through sponsorship that will flow into the planning phase and inform the whole process several years into the future. This would include:

- Revenue targets with balance of benefit in kind and cash if appropriate.
- If benefit in kind includes expertise, a list of the desired areas and expected benefits.
- Intended uses of the sponsorship money for any extra projects or development over and above supporting normal running costs.
- A list of other benefits, including specific audiences to be reached such as schools, local or national government, community leaders, etc.
- Desired and measurable outcomes such as growing awareness of the sport or activity, media exposure or enhanced facilities for athletes or performers.

? Why bother with a sponsorship strategy?

For many of us the strategy may be simply to go out and get some extra revenue. In other cases it might be considered rather late to devise a strategy since you are already in the market.

In both cases, however, it is worth doing as it means that any subsequent action fits in with the overall focus and direction that the organization wants to take. It should all be integrated with everything you want to do and your ambitions. Things change fast in organizations, and at present they seem to change faster than ever. People move on, and ideas that were very valuable and very relevant three years ago sometimes look rather stale when they are reviewed again.

A strategy is really an insurance policy for setting out what the thinking was, and what the goals were, so that people can refer to the original expectations. This helps to protect the organization and also us individually as practitioners and employees. It helps to protect our jobs because it shows the intelligence and logic that informed the decision to enter into sponsorship. Finally, any measurements or evaluation of the sponsorship, or of your own performance, make sense only if they can be put against some sort of background benchmark data.

Our experiences as a sponsorship agency and in working inside global brands tells us how real-life sponsors think, and the best ones are very clear about how important having a strategy is for them.

A survey by the European Sponsorship Association in Figure 6.2 shows that when sponsors were asked to name the biggest single factor to being successful in sponsorship, their top priority was "developing a strategy".

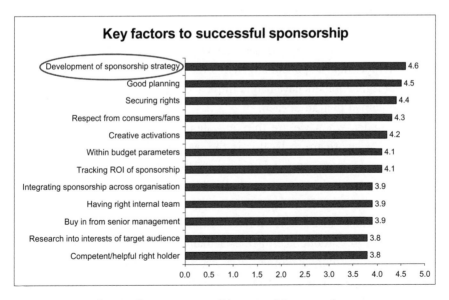

Figure 6.2 Key factors to successful sponsorship as seen by sponsors
(*Reproduced with permission of the European Sponsorship Association*)

We suggest that rights-holders should also put developing a sponsorship strategy high up on their levels of importance.

? Is sponsorship right for us?

It is quite legitimate to examine the impact that having sponsors would make on your organization, and in some cases it is important to limit the role sponsorship will play. In some rare cases it is acknowledged that the organization should not even be considering sponsorship at all. Table 6.2 gives a checklist when thinking about your own organization.

The next section looks at this increasingly common and beneficial development described above, where it is possible to get something in addition to just money, and where sponsors can bring something to organizations they do not currently have but is just as valuable as liquid cash.

Sponsors can give more than cash

We believe that the recession has accelerated a process that was probably already happening in sponsorship. The only good thing about the crisis has been that rights-holders have had to think a lot harder about other values that can be obtained instead of cash.

The model, when we are thinking about this, is the word "consideration", and what we mean by this is the overall value of what the sponsor is bringing. In most cases it is loaded on the left of Figure 6.3. Everyone likes money because it is extremely flexible and can be used in every possible way imaginable for the good of the organization. Increasingly, however, it is not possible to ask for, or receive, the cash that perhaps it was even a few years ago. Although companies actually sign numerically just as many deals as before, there is some anecdotal and statistical evidence to show that the average duration and value of deals has been falling, which many in the sponsorship selling business have learned the hard way in recent years.

Table 6.2 Checklist of risks

Risks to existing funding	One of the objections that sometimes appears internally, often in publicly funded bodies, is a fear about funding. Pressure on public money is forcing many bodies to consider repairing budget holes with commercial money.
	• The concern often voiced is that starting to get sponsorship, or significantly upgrading an existing low profile sponsorship programme, is going to affect the way public bodies or governments see the organization.
	• The worst case imagined is that by becoming more self-supporting it would be an argument for reduced public support. This is a legitimate fear for many organizations and worth exploring and recording at the strategy setting phase.
Internal changes: tools and resources required	Sponsorship is a very time consuming activity and issues to consider in setting the internal strategy include:
	• Who should be involved?
	• Who is going to take control and try to coordinate the programme?
	• Would it mean hiring extra staff, or using an outside agency?
	We recommend studying this area carefully following the three points below. Being realistic about the demands on staff time will help make sure everyone is comfortable from the outset with no nasty surprises coming down the track in the future.
	• Analysis of how different departments work together and co-ordinate activities. Bigger rights-holders may have advertising, PR and ticket sales departments which will need to work together.
	• What is required in order to approach, manage and fully exploit commercial sponsorship? An example being a sports team where one of the sponsorable assets is access to athletes or use of the venue or facility. Pre-planning saves potential conflicts between athletes and staff wanting to concentrate on preparing to compete and win and the commercial department who need access to those athletes.
	• Would this affect current HR deployment?
Tax, financial and political risks	Some of the issues that can raise their head are financial:
	• Sponsorship income can be treated differently by tax authorities. Some organizations for example have been caught by having to pay VAT on tickets or hospitality given out for free but seen as constituting a taxable benefit.
	• There are also rules on the hospitality and tickets that can be received by politicians, policy makers and corporate employees which may diminish the value of what you can offer. This varies country by country, but it can indeed be an issue, and needs specialist advice before going too far.

continued on next page ...

Table 6.2 (*continued*)

Internal conflicts	Another worry often expressed internally at this stage is the possibility of some sort of contamination by commercial sponsors, or in having unsuitable sponsors, especially in sensitive areas like snack food, alcohol or gambling. • Most organizations have some sort of policy about not taking tobacco or alcohol or firearms which are the obvious ones, but defining and discussing this issue and having a written policy signed and agreed is part of any sensible strategic review. This is not always the case in every single institution that we see but it is vital that the responsibility is shared and everything is accountable. • This is especially important in the very transparent world of NGOs and non-profit organizations which are still sometimes very sensitive internally to the idea of being influenced by a commercial sponsor. Having that written policy is good insurance for everyone inside the organization both now and in the future.
Is it just all about the money?	The ultimate question to be asked about why you are using sponsorship is "how does it fit into what we do as an organization or institution"? • Many of the internal objections come from an old fashioned view of sponsorship based on an era when sponsors gave cash in return for some exposure. We find these objections can be handled better by explaining that sponsors know that only by integrating deep into the sponsored property, and by being seen to have brought obvious benefit for both parties, will sponsorship ever be successful. • Once internal objectors or cynics see the potential that a corporate sponsor with a big PR machine can have on raising awareness of the event or activity that they love, we find they often begin to be enthused by the possibilities and become extremely helpful. • Showing how a sponsor can help by giving value over and above money also neutralizes an objection sometimes voiced inside an organization with such huge operating budgets that any revenue brought in by sponsorship is dwarfed in comparison.

So what do we do if we have a sponsor who says, "Well actually my budgets are down, I can't pay that much"? It does not have to be the end of the conversation, but might be the beginning of a new one, looking at other things that can balance up the diminished share of cash value as shown on the right hand side of Figure 6.3.

CASH
- Scheduled payments
- Performance bonuses

OTHER
- Value in kind
  - Personnel
  - Technology
  - Administrative resources
  - Materials provision
  - Specialist skills/expertise
- Marketing in kind
  - Database
  - Communications
  - Introductions
  - Brand enhancement
- Enhanced visitor experience

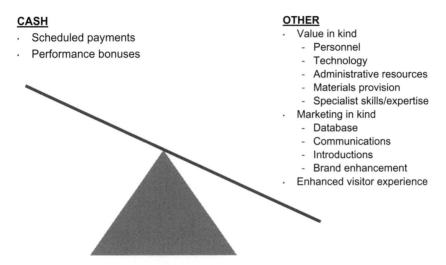

Figure 6.3 Balancing cash and other considerations

When switching to look at non-cash value there are two broad headings: Value in kind and Marketing in kind.

Value in kind

Receiving materials and product, as long as they are budget-relieving because they were needed anyway, is an obvious benefit. The most obvious examples are companies like Nestlé's Pure Life water sponsoring the Virgin London Marathon. The event thus saves on an item that it would have otherwise have had to purchase from its operating budget.

 Case Study: Nokia and the World Wildlife Fund

 Key learning point

- New technology has hugely widened the scope and capability of sponsorship agreements.

continued on next page ...

WWF and Nokia developed an intranet helping WWF store photographs online of current projects and endangered species. Previously this has been done in print and WWF were quick to point out the advantages of having such a partner: *"more flexible, real-time information from the field, interactive and more effective ... and also cheaper!"*

Graham Minton Head of Corporate Responsibility WWF

Action points

- Look carefully at how your organization uses IT or how it could use an enhanced package of software or hardware.
- Look for unique and attractive opportunities that would appeal to an IT company wanting to showcase its products.

Another good example is companies in the IT sector who can bring in incredible amounts of budget-relieving value to rights-holders and can also help to improve internal processes and efficiency. This is why companies such as HP, Intel and Dell and slightly less publicly well-known firms like SAP and AMD have all been Formula One racing sponsors. They have helped the teams with technology and skills (and also had the benefit of providing a very stimulating environment to develop their people and equipment in exceptionally short lead times). Indeed, value in kind can go much further as inside most sponsoring companies there is a fantastic range of human resources and specialist skills, which, if bought in commercially, would cost a very great deal. There are human resources, logistics, accounting and management professionals. Being open to this kind of support can ease the eventual negotiation of a deal and also tells the potential sponsor that you do understand the benefit for them of having their products showcased in a desirable setting and finding ways to reward their employees.

continued on next page ...

Marketing in kind

Marketing in kind takes advantage of the often considerable marketing and communication assets owned by sponsors which can be used to enhance the rights-holder's responsibilities. It feeds into the whole new idea of sponsorship, which is about being a platform, about engaging the consumer, and enriching the experience that the sponsor's customers can have. Sponsors will enter a sponsorship because it delivers them something they can then offer to their employees, customers or would-be customers.

 Case Study: Accenture's *"Intelligent Funding"* Model

 Key learning points

- A combination of cash and value-in-kind designed to maximize the value in the sponsorship and provide a business showcase for Accenture. This has been applied to relationships from the Royal Yachting Association, to Scottish Opera and the National Theatre.
- A model that appeals to Accenture as it challenges their employees to apply their business and management expertise outside their usual areas, and also provides the company with a platform to engage with employees and build a sense of pride.
- A model that generates discernable business benefit and gives Accenture a platform to discuss its sponsorships and showcase the organizations involved with clients, prospects and in the media.

Accenture's *Intelligent Funding* model is a combination of cash and value-in-kind work which has been successfully applied with various
continued on next page ...

organizations in the worlds of sport and culture that reflect the company's brand values of innovation and high performance, including the National Theatre, Scottish Opera, The Royal Shakespeare Company and the Royal Yachting Association.

Accenture works with such organizations to identify areas where they need help, where they don't have the necessary skills or budget to meet complex issues, and then provides the necessary expertise to create a viable solution. This model also provides Accenture with the opportunity to showcase its expertise and give its employees challenging work in fields in which they might not usually work. As a platform for employee engagement and motivation this is particularly useful.

Accenture has helped the National Theatre in more than just monetary terms, by looking at and assisting the National Theatre as a business entity, both in terms of its balance sheet and its operations. Accenture helped to optimize the National Theatre website and pricing structure by analysing the ebbs and flows of demand, enabling the theatre ultimately to sell more tickets. Accenture used analytical techniques to drill down into audience data and so help provide the theatre with a better understanding of its audiences in planning for the future. It has also created and installed The Big Wall – a large interactive screen for visual displays.

Accenture has also applied this model to the world of sailing, specifically Skandia Team GBR, the British Sailing Team and the Royal Yachting Association (RYA). Like all national governing bodies, the RYA was experiencing continual unpredictability on budgets through member churn. They found that people were joining the RYA and then leaving, perhaps only a year later. They wanted to understand more about this member attrition so Accenture helped them to analyse the problem and provide a solution. The RYA is at the sharp end of sailing with elite competition in the Olympics and Skandia Team GBR. It is

continued on next page ...

vital that every single selected athlete can best marshal their time and resources and focus on winning. Accenture put in place a performance management tool that enables the coaches and performance directors to monitor and measure all aspects of the sailors' performance and help them focus on winning.

For more information about Accenture and its approach to sponsorships in the UK, please visit http://www.accenture.com/Countries/UK/About_Accenture/Sponsorships

(*Reproduced with permission of Accenture*)

 ## Case Study: Deloitte Ignite

 ### Key learning point

• A five-year partnership to widen access to the Royal Opera House (ROH) worth £1.75 m and targeted at young professionals.

Deloitte partnered the Royal Opera House to challenge conventional perceptions of both parties and demonstrate innovation with a commitment to widening access to the arts. Deloitte was approached by the Royal Opera House as it recruits many young professionals and is one of the largest graduate employers in the UK – the prime audience for Deloitte Ignite. Apart from providing the funding, Deloitte is actively involved with the festival and has many different parts of the festival working with the Royal Opera House – from consultants, technology specialists to employee volunteers – to enhance Deloitte Ignite year on year.

continued on next page ...

Action point:

- Look inside your organization for areas and opportunities the sponsor can help strengthen. This helps you directly and provides the sponsor with wider credentials of their involvement beyond the cash investment.

(*Reproduced with permission of Deloitte*)

 Case Study: Quantum of Solace

 Key learning point:

- This is an extreme and high-profile example of the new trend of sponsors helping with promotion.

A James Bond film is one of the most highly sponsored properties in the world in terms of the number of companies that get involved, from Coca-Cola to Sony, Microsoft to car companies like Ford. These sponsors are not there to help MGM to fund the production of the film but to cross-sell the film and their involvement and rights of association as widely as possible. MGM needed to persuade distributors, pack cinemas, sell merchandise, DVDs, and video on demand, and the studio needed sponsors to help to soften the huge promotional budget. What is impressive is that these companies embedded their products deeply down into the film and actually made a functional point about the brand. For example, Ford knew that women actually buy more cars than men and so the Bond girl drives a small Ford Ka rather than an Aston Martin. Coca-Cola exploited their huge reach by making special edition bottles of Coke Zero, Zero 7.

continued on next page ...

Action points:

- Look inside your organization to see if increased awareness would be helpful or if there are any desired target audiences of yours that are not yet being reached.
- Be prepared to trade any shortfall in cash from the sponsor by having a clear idea of the non-cash promotional benefits you would like from a sponsor.

(?) Putting our organization in context: how do sponsors see us?

Perceptions of us within the potential sponsor marketplace

We always encourage sponsor seekers to step back a little and try to discover what images and feelings, if any, the outside world has of your organization or brand. This is important as sponsorship is an exchange of image attributes from the sponsored event or property to the sponsor. If you do not have a clear idea of your own image attributes and your own values, how can that possibly be sold later on to a sponsor? The key is to encapsulate what it is that you have uniquely that the sponsor could not obtain elsewhere.

At the very least, five minutes on Google, and especially Twitter (which is a great way to see how people feel about things), can help to provide direction on this. In fact this exercise is worth doing anyway because any sponsor even moderately interested will do exactly the same thing at a very early stage in deciding whether to look further or not.

Identify the audiences and networks with whom we could enable a sponsor to communicate

Sponsorship can be seen as an introduction made to a certain audience, a certain group of people associated with that sponsored property. We have to be able to explain in detail exactly what kind of people we are introducing them to in order to excite the sponsor. Your audiences and the networks that have been built up over time have much more value to potential sponsors than is often supposed.

When a group of sponsors in the USA were asked the question "Which of the following characteristics do you typically analyse when you are making a decision to sponsor?", the first one that came up was demographics.

What sponsors want to know is "exactly who are the people that you're bringing to me?" One of the things that can be done at this very early stage in the sponsorship process is to collect data to describe your audience or fans.

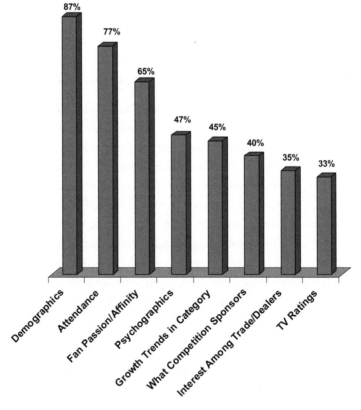

Figure 6.4 Data considered most important by sponsors (*Reproduced with permission of* IEG)

Even a simple self-run spectator study can generate information that will later help to lift a proposal above the competition. A sample size of 200 is generally considered big enough, and although prices vary by country they can be bought for around £7,000 to £9,000. They can, of course, also be carried out for less using volunteers or students from the local university.

Case Study: F.I.M. Motocross World Championships

An example of the kind of data that can be produced from a quick spectator survey is that the World Motocross Championship in 2006 were able to claim that 67% of their fans at the track were between 15 and 39 years old, were 80% male and that 87% would either "definitely" or "possibly" buy brands that sponsor their sport.

Not only this, but Youthstream, the agency who market the series, were able to prepare interesting data for future sponsorship proposals by giving information not only on who the fans are, in terms of sex and age, but, for example:

- How many times do they buy a mobile phone a year?
- How many holidays do they have?
- Would they buy a sponsor's products if they backed this activity?
- What kind of companies would be suitable sponsors?

(With permission of Youthstream)

 Comparing competitors' and international best practice

The experiences of similar institutions or events that you might perhaps see as competition often contain some valuable lessons and should not be wasted. Areas to look at during this process of getting your own house in order are shown in Table 6.3.

Table 6.3 Competitors and action

Competitors	Action
Who are our competitors?	• If a sponsor is looking at you it is likely they are also considering other similar opportunities. Make sure your knowledge of the market is as good as or better than that of any other prospect.
Do they have sponsors?	• What do they offer and can we copy and enhance this? • How long have they kept their sponsors for? • Would their sponsors be good for us?
How did they get sponsors and when?	• This is not easy to find out but worth trying as the same approach could be refined and improved for your benefit also.
What's their retention rate like?	• Some specialist resource such as The World Sponsorship Monitor (TWSM) published by IFM Sports Marketing Surveys can help you research, and a simple way is to go online looking at your competitors' materials from a few years before to see any pattern in their array of sponsors.
How do they service them?	• Often hard to discern from the outside but worth exploring anecdotally with any contacts you can find.
What did they pay?	• One of the biggest challenges in sponsorship is understanding how much sponsors are paying for similar rights. • Sponsorship is a very un-transparent market and pricing information is hard to come by and usually highly confidential. There are some sources like TWSM or agencies with a feeling for the market, and if you are fortunate sometimes you may find some information online.

Modern sponsor needs and insights

We are beginning to consider how our strategy must take account of the sponsor's needs, and any insights into what modern sponsors expect are very valuable at this stage to enable attractive features to be built into your offering. Every day in our work we see the trends outlined and being aware of them will help you to adapt your strategy to the modern sponsorship marketplace. We will look at how sponsors can be interested in providing mentoring opportunities to reward valued employees, the new interest in grassroots or community sponsorship and, lastly, the desire for sponsorship to provide special "money can't buy experiences" for customers, employees or would-be customers.

The rise of mentoring

Mentoring typically means the chance for employees of a company to give their skills to another organization. This is becoming more and more important, especially as the cash/in kind balance changes. Companies are seeing an incredible value in giving something back to their employees in terms of creating different and stimulating experiences. They do this to:

- stimulate professional talents by putting them in new environments
- prevent boredom and people leaving
- build pride in the company
- demonstrate good corporate citizenship and brand values
- build a point of difference and to attract recruits
- make up for an inability to offer significant salary increases.

UNESCO is a good example of a body that enjoys enormous assistance from their range of sponsors, which is very wide. They are able to bring in lawyers, disaster relief specialists, and logistics experts which would literally cost a fortune if paid for.

HSBC, who are a leading edge global sponsor, had a scheme called *Investing in Nature*, a partnership with the World Wildlife Fund, Botanic Gardens Conservation International (BGCI) and Earthwatch where 2,000 HSBC employees worked on vital conservation research projects around the world. On return they briefed colleagues and carried out a local environmental project, relating their experience in the field to their local environment and their role in their own communities and at work. Although it may seem, at first glance, to be not a very natural partnership for a major global bank to be with these prestigious NGOs, both sides have worked incredibly successfully together for a very long time and the scheme led to the 2007 HSBC Climate Partnership with The Climate Group, Earthwatch, Smithsonian Tropical Research Institute (STRI) and WWF. Employees reportedly developed key skills, such as leadership and teamwork, with positive effects on staff morale, retention and recruitment.

Grassroots sponsorship

Another trend we are seeing is the idea of sponsors trying to be relevant to local communities. Most elite level sponsorships in, for example, major club soccer or the Olympics, now nearly always have some grassroots or community element built in. In non-sport areas, some examples that have won sponsorship awards recently come from BT in the UK gaining enormous goodwill in local communities by giving them broadband access for the first time, and Turkcell in Turkey helping rural young women to adapt in a very changeable, modernizing society. McDonald's do this very effectively, as we see below.

 Case Study: McDonald's and Youth Volunteering Charity "V"

 Key learning points:

- Most brands, even if global names, also have local roots and communities that they need to nurture.
- Look to build in or up-scale ways in which a sponsor could use you to get involved with a local community they need to reach.

McDonald's is one of the truly global brands but it is also a local business in almost every town around the world, so for them having a link at a grassroots level makes sense. As well as being a FIFA World Cup sponsor and The FA's Community Partner they worked alongside "V" to address a concern affecting many of their customers – that of a lack of good-quality coaching which was affecting their children's ability to enjoy playing soccer.

The scheme offers leadership and volunteering opportunities through football, and working alongside The FA, McDonald's aimed to

continued on next page ...

recruit at least 900 extra young volunteers, aged between 16 and 25, to deliver at least one year of voluntary coaching. This was backed by 43 McDonald's football festivals across England and donations of over £2m of kit and equipment. McDonald's married up their elite and grassroots soccer activity and also usefully countered the fast-food and obesity arguments by proving that they were enabling young people to take more exercise. Lastly, they gained credibility in using well-known soccer players to endorse the programme.

(Reproduced with permission of McDonald's)

"Money Can't Buy" experiences

In the "experience economy" the great power of sponsorship is the ability to create highly prized unique experiences by leveraging the assets imaginatively as in the three case studies below.

 Case Study: FedEx European Rugby Cup Sponsorship – FedEx Rugby Dream Day

 Key learning points:

- Try to identify in the strategy setting phase what it is that the sponsor can obtain only from you that they in turn can use to leverage the sponsorship programme.
- Companies are looking for a unique – "money can't buy" experience for customers to leverage sponsorship investment.

FedEx is a sponsor of the European Rugby Cup. FedEx Rugby Dream Day is an online game that engages rugby fans and offers a unique prize
continued on next page ...

to the winner – the cornerstone of which is the opportunity to carry the Heineken Cup Trophy from pitch-side to the winner's podium in front of 80,000 fans. This, together with world class VIP hospitality to the final, receiving 2 signed team shirts and getting a full-page personal profile in the final match day programme ensures that the winner really does receive a unique – money can't buy – experience.

(Reproduced with permission of FedEx)

 Case Study: Telecom, Adidas and The New Zealand All Blacks

 Key learning points:

- Two sponsors of New Zealand's legendary rugby team have been very successful in understanding that buying the sponsorship allows them to create "money can't buy" experience for their customers.

Telecom New Zealand really made the most out of their sponsorship of the country's legendary All Blacks rugby team and in doing so made sure the fan was the centre of the experience and the set of rights they had bought. Their core All Blacks campaign is called BackingBlack. BackingBlack is an All Blacks supporters club that is enabled by Telecom and about uniting fans and connecting them to the team – be it virtually though backingblack.co.nz, physically through money-can't-buy experiences or through prize draws to win tickets to All Blacks games. Imagine the power of having All Black players personally call subscribers to tell them they had won match tickets, with one winner even going to Paris to watch the team play in France. The players are made available to attend events like cooking lunch with fans and coverage of these events is leveraged through television, press and online sources like YouTube.

(Reproduced with permission of Telecom New Zealand)

Case Study: Carling and *Cold Beer Amnesty* at Music Festivals

Key learning points:

- Beer marketers have to overcome fierce brand loyalty based on emotional engagement rather that product differentials to encourage consumers to switch brands.
- Carling based their activation of their sponsorship of music festivals on a genuine insight to a problem, providing a solution that added real value to consumers experience at festivals.

As musicians see their recording revenues shrink there has been a growth in live music with massive audiences at festivals and venues all over the world. Over the last two decades, this area has become as appealing to brands who want to connect with consumers as sport as it offers the same benefit of access to passionate, committed fans.

Beer brand Carling are active in both sport and music sponsorship and they know that switching brand preference in the beer market is one of the hardest challenges in marketing as people have strong feelings and loyalties to individual beers. But the pay off for encouraging switchers is great exactly because of this loyalty.

Carling has been at the forefront of the music sponsorship for the last decade. Historically they have been headline sponsors of the Reading and Leeds festivals, Carling Academies and more recently as the official beer of Isle of Wight Festival, V Festival and RockNess. But as the marketplace became more saturated with many brands competing for share of voice a simple association with music was not enough. They had to be more creative in how they communicated with consumers, giving a tangible benefit to their role at festivals that provided creditability to their association.

So Carling – through the experiential agency, Cake – used their knowledge in the festival arena to consider problems that festival goers experience when on site. They then looked to provide a solution to a problem that would provide a real benefit to festival goers.

The problem with music festivals is that you carry your beer from the local supermarket and 24 hours in a hot, stuffy tent ensures they have warmed up and are unpleasant to drink. The best way to drink lager is ice-cold. So to provide the best drinking experience possible Cake came up with an insightful idea called the *Cold Beer Amnesty*. At Isle of Wight, V Festival and RockNess, festival goers could bring their warm beer and swap it for an ice-cold can of Carling. This tackles brand allegiance, but in a soft way. It says: "*We forgive you for drinking other brands and we are here to help you and add value to your festival experience*". This is exactly the tone that should be taken by all successful sponsorships.

Action point: Look for similar opportunities within your own inventory where the sponsor can add value for your fans and the event while at the same time achieving their own marketing aims.

(Reproduced by permission of Carling)

 # Key take-outs

- What you are selling is not sponsorship; you are selling a tool for a sponsor to undertake their marketing objectives.
- Modern sponsors have gone a long way beyond just buying logo exposure.
- You must dig deep to find assets that will allow sponsors to connect directly and genuinely with the people that you bring to them, and you must know everything about these groups.
- At the initial strategy stage don't forget the built-in value you have of previous or existing sponsors, and your image or values.
- Take head-on the downsides of sponsorship and make sure that all within your organization have aired their opinion, had the strategy explained to them and feel comfortable in signing off on going out to attract sponsors.

- Look to see where you can find assets appealing to the new generation of sponsors, such as opportunities for employee engagement, mentoring or offering a direct route to a local community.
- Companies can bring so much more than just cash. Look around to see where you could benefit from expertise and resources in marketing, promotion, consultancy, IT and other goods and services.

Summary

- Good preparation and sponsorship strategies lead to more successful sales, happier sponsors and saving money and time renewing those sponsors.
- You will benefit by working in a more harmonious environment, more supportive of sponsorship and with a clear understanding of the objectives of sponsorship and the desired benefits that will insure you against internal stresses both now and in a few years' time.
- The next chapter, Essential Sales Preparation, will help you to build on this firm foundation when constructing your sponsor hierarchy, the benefits packages, the pricing structure, and everything you need as you move towards the selling phase.

CHAPTER 7

ESSENTIAL SALES PREPARATION

 ## Overview

This chapter builds on Chapter 6 which concerned sponsorship strategy and setting a proper course into which everything else will feed later on. Knowing what is wanted from sponsorship as an organization will ultimately help to make the sales or to upgrade the sales process if that is what is required.

The main point here is that being well prepared makes a huge difference to your chances of standing out from the crowd of sponsorship proposals. This chapter covers:

- Getting in the frame of mind of looking at yourself from the sponsor's point of view.
- An Asset Checklist Tool, which lists some of the assets that might be found and some hints on where to find other assets that perhaps were not previously obvious.
- How to put a valuation on those assets: how much is your sponsorship worth?
- How to set the price of what you are offering to the market.
- Advice about how to construct the hierarchy of rights and benefits that are being offered to sponsors, and how to make it work for you and ultimately for your sponsors.

- What's in a name? Title and presenting sponsorships.
- New trends you should be aware of as you prepare to sell.

▼ Look at yourself from the sponsor's point of view

In Chapter 1 we considered how sponsorship is defined by the International Chamber of Commerce as a commercial agreement. Everyone agrees that a sponsorship is a commercial activity for mutual benefit but what does that actually mean? It means that what you are selling to a sponsor is not sponsorship; it's not your event or passion that is of interest in itself as the sponsor will see it simply as a tool for themselves. When those taking a decision in a sponsoring company look at your proposal, they will be asking themselves:

- What can they do with it?
- How is it going to help them do their job?
- How is it going to help with what that brand is trying to do?

Saying that you are a marketing tool is not meant to be pejorative; you are not going to be treated badly, it is simply the perspective that the sponsor is going to have. That is why this chapter helps you to try to look at your assets from the sponsor's point of view. If anyone in your organization holds some rather old-fashioned views about sponsorship, it has now gone far beyond putting up logos and boards, and maybe having some hospitality and tickets and an exchange of cash. The idea that sponsorship is some sort of donation because you are worthy no longer applies. Nor is sponsorship a cheap replacement for advertising. Sponsorship is not comparable to advertising and, in any case, it is not (in most, but not all cases) particularly cheap when compared to a straight media buy.

- If you try to sell exposure to the sponsor by comparing it to the cost of media buying, you are nearly always going to lose.

- Sponsorship should be so much more than merely a way of getting airtime or exposure.

Sponsorship has become much more sophisticated and, in general, sponsors have a fairly clear idea about what they want from you. What is happening now reflects a bigger change in society, which is that brands and companies have to actually stand for something. It's not just the product that people buy, as the actual product and its quality are now givens. What people expect is that the company actually stands for something, and that the brand means something. As an example, brands like Apple, Rolex, BMW or Nike have an almost emotional connection with consumers. This is why sponsorship has really grown, not just as an alternative to advertising, and not just something that can be bought off-the-shelf, but rather something that has to help with what the company is trying to achieve with the brand. Companies are now working in an integrated way which involves their PR, sales and marketing departments, in communicating their brand.

- More and more is the hat being passed around inside a company to raise the budget to pay your sponsorship fee.
- This is important because later on, when dealing with sponsors, you will be dealing not with a single person or department but with the company as a whole. This is why it is so important to have organized your assets sufficiently to appeal to more than one department within a company.

Organize your assets to appeal

Later in the book it will be demonstrated that good preparation is absolutely vital in selling sponsorship if you want to stand out from the masses of sponsorship seekers, especially in researching individual industries and brands when at the stage of writing tailor-made proposals. This pre-sales stage of organizing what you have to sell demands equally solid preparation to make your company ultimately more attractive than the opposition. The hard truth is that a company like Red Bull in one country alone can receive 300 separate sponsorship proposals every week – or 50 or 60 a day. This shows just how eye-catching you must be in your approach to get noticed.

Failure to prepare adequately is one of the principal reasons for a proposal to be rejected. You really must work internally at this stage to make sure that you have something attractive and special to sell.

One of the things noticed about successful people in all walks of life is that, generally, they seem to spend a lot of unseen time getting things absolutely right before they go public. The Abraham Lincoln quote we used in Chapter 2 of this book sums up equally well the approach we should all bear in mind when thinking about selling sponsorship.

> "If I had eight hours to chop down a tree, I would spend six hours sharpening my axe."
>
> *Abe Lincoln*

Now is the time to think very carefully about what could possibly be of value to a sponsor if you are to start making really top-class, standout proposals. In this chapter you can imagine gathering all your ingredients together in a kitchen store cupboard to enable you to start making individual recipes that can be devised to cater for the tastes of those individual companies and brands that have been identified in the research phase.

To continue the food analogy, we do not think anyone would ever make a dish by just throwing in every ingredient in the store cupboard, thinking that because each in itself is good, the resulting dish will be appetizing. Different sponsors have different tastes, and the ingredients that may be more prominent for some may not be required at all for others. It does make sense, however, to carry out a stocktake of every single thing you have to ensure that you know the ingredients and the combinations that are ultimately possible to suit different brands and product sectors.

- Gather all the ingredients in your kitchen.
- But combine only the right ones to cater for each sponsors individual taste.

The next section looks at the sponsorship assets that are typically sold as part of most sponsorship packages. Not each one will be right for you; some of them may be things you simply do not have, but hopefully you will have some assets that are unique to you and thus create value. However, the idea is to give reassurance to the sponsor that you have looked at all possibilities, and can provide some ideas where you can perhaps unlock extra value.

Standing back and thinking about sponsorship, the previous chapter encouraged you to make an asset inventory based on three very broad asset areas which are of benefit to sponsors, and is why people buy sponsorship.

- Connection with a target group
- Exposure
- Image transfer

Always remember your background thinking as you gather up your assets.

Table 7.1 gives a typical collection of some of the assets that are seen to be included in the sponsorship proposals that we see every day.

Table 7.1 Asset checklist tool

Media exposure and coverage	• Nearly always seen in every proposal. It must be described, measured and maximized in the most professional, truthful and accurate way possible. Remember that many people reading your proposals live and breathe media for a living, and clumsy or misleading descriptions of media benefits are both too common and extremely irritating.
	• Upgrade your list of exposure sources (posters, Twitter, Facebook, websites, brochures, etc) and try to find reliable up-to-date figures on attendance, press, online TV and media coverage.
Inclusion in all press releases and media activities	• This is a given, and a minimum courtesy to the sponsor, but a low value asset as press will rarely report on the event's sponsors.
PR campaign tailored to sponsor's special interest media	• This is more valuable and shows evidence of thinking about the sponsor's industry or the brand's need to communicate to specific media and engage with their own target audience.

continued on next page ...

Table 7.1   (continued)

Media contacts, sampling to media	• It is sometimes forgotten that properties, especially sports and arts properties, frequently have quite good relationships with journalists. It is not possible with every brand, but being able to exploit the relationship even further by putting a product into the hands of media and sampling is a very powerful benefit as media like nothing more than being treated well!
Proposed advertising	• Not all, but many, properties pay for some sort of advertising. Therefore it makes sense to offer first right of refusal to a potential or existing sponsor to join in on that advertising if possible.
Ticket/event brochure promotions	• A basic benefit.
Right to use your logos	• Most events or organizations have a logo, and depending on its perceived value and whether you can be seen to be giving endorsements, it might be an appropriate benefit to be offered.
Availability of speakers for sponsor's functions	• A very important aspect of sponsorship is that music, arts and sports are things people are genuinely interested in and therefore you have a pool of talented individuals who can be offered up to sponsors for functions.
Use of property/venue for sponsor events, customer relations, product launches, etc	• Some properties are fortunate in having something rather special, such as owning a stadium or theatre for example, and this is an asset that should be made to work hard for both you and the sponsor.
Access to mailing lists and opportunity to run database drawing promotion	• Sometimes there are data protection issues, but it is always worthwhile building up a database of fans as sponsors want the ability to contact a niche audience with a proven avidity for the activity in question. • Competitions or offers which harness this enthusiasm are ideal for database generating. Sports enthusiasts are one of the few groups in the world still happy to take part in surveys or fill in forms online!
Business-to-business benefits	• Something not done often enough is looking at the opportunity for sponsors to do business with co-sponsors through workshops or other types of hard work from the rights-owner in helping to bring businesses together and in making suggestions as to where they could be benefiting each other.

continued on next page ...

Table 7.1 *(continued)*

Employee engagement/ mentoring	• Something seen much more in sponsorship today is that companies are looking to give something back to their employees. This is especially true in hard times when companies are looking for non-cash rewards. • This is well worth thinking about during the initial planning of what assets you might be able to offer. Companies like HSBC, Accenture, or Deloitte look for something original for their employees to give them the stimulation of using their skills in a different environment.
Product placement	• Always look for ways that sponsors can somehow integrate their product or services into the centre of the action that you are offering. • If done properly this adds authenticity and credibility which will strengthen the impact of the sponsorship.
Merchandising rights	• Some properties have objects like T-shirts or other merchandise and a sponsor could be offered co-branding, or some sort of licensing – or simply bulk buy them as giveaways for their own use.
Endorsement of a sponsor	• Accepting sponsorship could be seen as a form of endorsement, but it may be possible to make this formal. Some properties, especially public or publicly funded bodies, may however have rules preventing this.
Provision of content for sponsor's website and social media	• Companies value good content for their websites and other online channels. You may have something interesting and unique which enables you to provide something that the sponsor was unable to source before.
Onsite sampling	• Sampling is fairly straightforward and is rightly seen in a lot of proposals.
Tie in cause/ community relations, CSR efforts	• The last few years have seen companies trying to engage at a local level by building in a connection to a city where they are a big employer, or to build on their CSR policy in reaching groups like children, the disabled or minorities. • Remember that CSR budgets are often separate from sponsorship and so represent a tempting source of funds. • However avoid the trap of saying "spend money with us and look good". People concerned with CSR inside a company know that CSR is about how a company makes its money, not just how it spends its money.

(?) How much should we ask for the sponsorship?

This section deals with how to approach one of the hardest things in sponsorship, which is how much to charge for your offering.

Most people have experienced some headaches in getting the pricing right, whether designing a brand new package or upgrading an existing offering, and a number of ways are used to estimate how much a sponsorship is worth:

- The event budget
- Benchmark with other events
- Make a proper assets audit and evaluation

The event budget

We see a lot of proposals giving many pages of great detail on the exact budget for the event, right down to things such as security, cleaning and hiring generators. Are the people producing these proposals hoping that, because it looks so credible and professionally organized, the sponsor will be impressed and will equate the costs to the rights-holder with the value for them? The truth is that no sponsor is concerned with your internal budget. It adds no credibility at all. Their main interest is in the value they get from you as a company or as a brand.

Benchmark with other events

So how is a sponsorship valued? One way is to have a good look at the marketplace, but the problem is that sponsorship is a very un-transparent market, and is one of the few that the internet has not yet opened up. The problem is what economists call asymmetric pricing information. This means that the buyer and the seller have access to very different information about how much the item is worth. Generally, sponsors have a fairly firm grip on how much they are prepared to pay, but sponsorship sellers have considerably less idea.

To try to level the playing field, some industry sources are available, such as magazines like *The World Sponsorship Monitor (TWSM)* produced by IFM Sports Marketing Surveys, and there are occasionally news reports about how much a sponsorship, especially a major one, is worth. But it is still very difficult, and is not like the housing market where an estate agent can say, "Well, a house in the same road sold for $400,000 recently so therefore yours should achieve a similar price." However, at least do your best to get a feel for the market.

Make a proper assets audit and evaluation

The ideal route for most properties is to have a proper, preferably independent, audit of what is on offer. This is worthwhile for three reasons:

- It gives confidence inside the sponsor's organization that the sum being demanded is justified (remember that in the minds of most salesmen there tends to be a feeling they are asking for too much money, so if that fear can be removed it should improve sales).
- When it comes to talking to sponsors, professional negotiators will usually tell you that having a benchmark or a "stick in the sand", in the form of a third-party valuation, is an effective way of conducting and easing a negotiation. Even if your potential sponsor is sceptical about the valuation, it is still an effective starting point for jointly exploring the value of what is being offered.
- It shows willingness on your part to think about the benefits being proposed in an analytical manner rather than based purely on intuition or guesswork.

But exactly how is a valuation of a sponsorship property reached? Figure 7.1 below shows the steps in *Sponsorship Consulting*'s own valuation model.

Impacts

Refer to all possible sources of exposure. For example, a valuation for an exhibition at a gallery included:

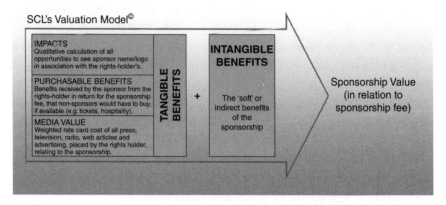

Figure 7.1 *Sponsorship Consulting's* valuation model

- *Signage* – Directional signage (A4 size). Entrance banner, signage in the galleries, souvenir guide book, pocket plan leaflet.
- *Print* – language neutral guide (new guide).
- *VIP Dinner* – directional signage, table plans, boards, sponsor statement board, invitation reply cards.

Purchasable benefits

These are things that could be bought by anyone so wishing, and therefore have a precise market value. In the case of the gallery this would include:

- 1 × "at cost" event (up to the value of $8,000);
- 100 × complimentary tickets for temporary museum exhibitions;
- 4 × opportunities for behind the scenes tours;
- 2 × opportunities for early morning tours with the Director of the Museum;
- weekend family days;
- 2 × opportunities to engage staff through adult learning;
- 3 × opportunities a year to engage a partner school through education programme;
- guided tours for company VIPs.

Media value

In the case of the gallery this included editorial coverage in national and regional press, paid advertising on the city's transport system, and one television appearance in the regional news.

Most valuations in the commercial world are based on the future value (usually revenue) accruing from the asset in question. In sponsorship, this is usually done by a mixture of tangible market equivalent benefits and intangible benefits, as set out below.

Tangible (has a monetary value)

- Media exposure: Equivalent advertising cost
- Tickets/hospitality: Alternative purchase cost; Scarcity – premium
- Database access: List purchase prices
- Meeting facilities: Conference room hire
- Brand ambassadors: Celebrity speaker fees
- Sampling: Commercial rentals; Display kiosk creation costs

Tangible means anything that you can go out and buy, so making it much easier to find the individual prices. For example, media exposure can be bought over the counter through the sales desk in a TV channel or a magazine. There is a great debate inside sponsorship about media exposure being considered equal to advertising, and counting towards the value of a sponsorship. Most sponsors discount it down; McDonald's, for example, allegedly take it down by as much as 90%, as exposure and awareness are not of primary value to their mature and omnipresent brand.

However, for the purposes of evaluation, and even though it may be discounted, it is advisable to calculate a tangible figure on what media coverage is actually generated. The same thing applies to tickets, but this is simpler as all tickets have a set face price. If you are able to offer some kind of database, the ability to evaluate that can be obtained from the rate cards of companies that do that for a living. Valuing a venue is easy, as prices for venue hire, signage inside venues, conferences and events are plentiful online. There are also rate cards for speakers, for direct marketing, and for sampling and kiosks at events.

Something that is a little difficult is to try to value the intangibles on top of the tangibles.

Intangible (value is non-financial)

- Transferable brand attributes
- Property prestige
- Quality of delivery
- Convenience of location
- Credible brand endorsement
- Category exclusivity
- Strength of shared goals
- Networking opportunities
- Exclusivity of access
- Uncluttered environment
- Impact on recruitment
- Political/community goodwill

The essence of intangible value is how much is it worth for a company to augment its brand attributes in conjunction with your own?

- What is it you are offering?
- What is the prestige?
- What is special about what you are offering?
- What sort of experience is a sponsor going to have and how is this going to benefit the customers?
- What is different about this?

One intangible benefit that appears in polls of sponsors in Europe and the USA is the appreciation by sponsors of exclusivity. As ever, it comes back to the same thing – are you offering something unique? Is it something that a sponsor should buy because you are the only supplier?

Although having current or previous sponsors can give a sponsor confidence, the value of co-sponsors has to be balanced by the fact that this might increase the clutter and general feeling that you are in a crowded marketplace. The trend now is to try to make things tidy by having as few sponsors as possible but a much deeper relationship with each of them.

Another area that can be factored in is that sponsorship is a very flexible tool. It is not always only about increasing sales, it can be used to reach audiences such as politicians, investors, potential employees and universities and NGOs, and it should be possible to take a view on how much value results from this.

Setting the price

It is valuable to have these kinds of numbers, and by combining the two it is possible to look at the ratio between tangible and intangible.

- A minimum cash fee based on the value of the tangible benefits offered
- Add a sum in recognition of intangibles, associated benefit, etc.; 25% of tangibles is a good starting place for brands, 100% of tangibles for rightsholders – that is why it is a negotiation!
- Create a bonus programme for exceeding agreed service levels, e.g.
  - Brand exposure via TV coverage
  - Number of sponsor mentions by rights-holder personnel
  - Brand awareness/brand attributes targets
  - New database records collected.

One way of presenting the valuation could be to say: "These are the tangible benefits but what we are offering is sponsorship, where intangibles like emotion and image transfer are key value drivers." It is good, however, to start with the tangibles because they are a hard benefit and you can show the rigour of your analysis and professionalism. This is a good way to start the negotiation because you have a process to go through. We generally find that sponsors do not agree with the figure of tangibles and that the starting point will go down. However, at least we have something solid to discuss rather than just exchanging subjective opinions about where the true value lies.

The next step is using the tangible value to come to an agreement about the intangibles, and experience shows that brands and sponsor seekers estimate this to be between 25% and 100% of the tangible. The skill is negotiating a satisfactory resolution between the two views.

Sharing the risks and rewards

When it comes to negotiations, it may be useful during this sales preparation phase to plan ahead for having a policy on a trend that the recession has exaggerated. Hard-pressed sellers have been enabling deals to go through by sharing the risks and rewards. This is most usually seen with benefits like exposure. This applies particularly to sports teams, e.g. if a soccer team is going to be promoted to the Premier League, that normally means that the value would rise considerably. Even for much smaller properties it is possible to say "If we over-achieve, would you consider a payment to reward us for the benefits we have brought to both sides?" Sometimes it can be measured by such things as how frequently a verbal mention of a sponsor is made, or perhaps it is to do with surveys on awareness, or, in more tangible metrics, it can be the number of new customer records that have been transferred.

Creating a sponsor hierarchy

Creating a structure to propose to sponsors – and which also works for you – is another tricky area in sponsorship. Everyone from global mega-events to community events struggles with this, and good preparation at this stage can save various problems later.

Maybe you have a new event or perhaps you have never had sponsors before – or only small sponsors that you have inherited and are wondering how to fit them into an upgraded structure? In all cases the main issues are:

- The need to prepare exactly what the key rights are for Title Sponsor, Official Sponsor, Official Supplier, etc.
- Will it be "cluttered" with other sponsors?
- Category Exclusivity for sponsors. Is this something that can be offered?

At this preparation stage it is advisable to think exactly what the benefits are for the individual tiers of sponsors and how they can stand out in the "clutter". One way to overcome the problem is to challenge one of the biggest clichés in sponsorship ...

- Avoid Gold, Silver, Bronze packages!

 Sponsors see so many of these offers that they call it "precious metal fatigue" and Boutros Boutros, Divisional Senior Vice-President of Corporate Communications, Emirates, speaking in 2010 put it very well. While not perhaps referring directly to precious metal fatigue he proves the need to communicate why the sponsor is there:

> "As a sponsor, I am not gratified by such offers, because at the end of the day my intention is to stand out and have a voice. Seeing my logo, however, along with 50 other logos of brands and companies does not serve my strategy to distinguish the name of my brand."

We accept the argument sometimes made that Gold or Platinum shows a sponsor is in the prestige top level but Gold, Silver, Bronze will not help you stand out and using them will make life harder for you. Even if you avoid boring or annoying the potential sponsor enough for them to look at the packages, modern sponsors do not negotiate on package levels that have been set in advance. They will cherry pick, only taking those assets in which they are interested. Worse still, they will go in at the lowest level and then spend the money they have saved on activating the sponsorship to get more value and prominence – more perhaps than some of your other sponsors who are paying more.

Our apologies to anyone who is still using "precious metals", but we intend to help you to find a real life structure that is logical and clear. The answer is to use descriptive titles with exact definitions for sponsors – such as Title Sponsor, Official Sponsor, and Official Supplier, etc.

A good example comes from the FIFA World Cup:

- FIFA Partner (sponsors associating with FIFA globally over a long period)
- FIFA World Cup sponsor (sponsors associating with FIFA globally over one World Cup)

- National Supporter (sponsors associating with FIFA nationally over one World Cup)

Figure 7.2 shows an example of an event and tells you exactly what everyone is going to have. If we look at Tier One, the Official Sponsors, this title enables you to tell sponsors: "You will have exclusivity, you will be the only soft drinks sponsor." It also recognizes that the benefits a soft drinks sponsor wants, such as sampling or exposure perhaps, are quite different to those, say, of a bank, who will want business generation and hospitality. It is not a question of offering the same thing to everybody, but rather it is tailoring the offer to each individual industry segment. Also worth emulating is the idea of giving the main sponsors "ownership" of a sub-event or activity. This gives them a second front for leveraging their sponsorship and reaching their target audi-

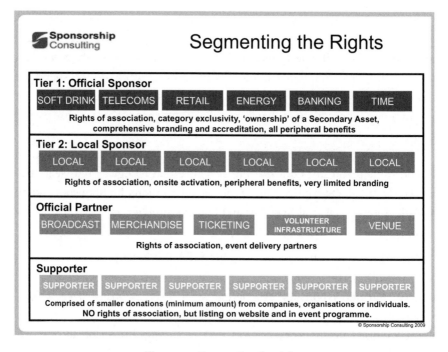

Figure 7.2 Segmenting the rights

ence. For example, they could have an online presence exclusive to them, perhaps a lounge at the event, or offer a play area for children. Another example would be sponsoring a special award within a film festival for instance.

The recognition of the different needs of, say, an Official Sponsor and a Local Sponsor avoids a problem commonly faced in designing sponsorship packages. Many of us have found ourselves rehashing the same set of benefits, trying desperately to keep the top tier with a markedly superior package without scalping the lower levels of any residual value. This is why you often find that the Silver and Bronze levels are almost carbon copies of the Gold, and there is little differentiation between the various layers.

Some people say to us: "Well that's okay for a big event but ours is so small this simply wouldn't work for us." However, this approach does indeed produce benefits when scaled down to smaller properties. Not only that, but remember that smaller events do have some benefits over larger ones, including:

- Fewer sponsors, more connection, closer relationship, more creativity.
- Fewer sponsors require less time and money spent looking after them. Your relationship will allow you to get closer to them and as a result of this perhaps have a better relationship with scope for creative ideas to come from both sides.
- Small events can confer the benefits of extreme passion and fan avidity to the sponsor. According to IFM Sports Marketing Surveys' UK-based sponsorship brand tracker Sponsatrak, 14% of sports fans agreed to the proposition that *"I am more inclined to purchase a product from a corporation that sponsors than one that doesn't"*. This may not sound much perhaps, but the Holy Grail of marketing is to make someone's propensity to purchase change, so if you get 14% of even a small group of people to buy or switch brands, there are some immediate business benefits.
- Finally it is believed that in creating very highly structured packages, and trying to defend the system that you have built up, you must also recognize the reality of things and be very flexible. The key is rigour in your sales preparation and knowing exactly what you've got, thus giving sponsors what they want.

Prepare yourself for dealing with benefit in kind

We looked at benefit in kind (BIK) and marketing in kind (MIK) in Chapter 6 and many rights-holders use a mix of benefit in kind to compensate for cash, especially now that budgets are much tighter. It can be very effective, but prior to selling, here are some general warnings:

- Only accept MIK or especially BIK if it is something that will relieve an expense line already in the budget.
- Do not do it because you have approached a sponsor that has offered a product or a service that you do not actually need, but you do not want to turn the sponsor down.
- This will increase your sponsor servicing costs and add to the clutter and devalue the field for everybody else.

Title and presenting sponsorships

It was said earlier that a top sponsor should have recognizably the best package. If you are able to offer the title of your property or event, there is no doubt that it can be a great asset and inducement. A title sponsor can have some significant advantages in providing a considerable amount of revenue and cutting your costs on multiple sponsor servicing, but can also present you with some quite serious challenges.

However, title sponsors need to have a manifestly more powerful package than anybody else, so there may be problems from other sponsors lower down the order because the title sponsor can take up some of their oxygen.

 Case Study: Maruti and Cricket World Cup 2007

 Key learning points:

- Cricket is an incredibly popular sport in India and huge sums of money are commonly paid by sponsors. Many were surprised, however, when the Indian car maker Maruti agreed a one million US

continued on next page ...

dollar sponsorship deal for the Cricket World Cup website cricket-worldcup.com. Maruti apparently wanted to link the modern high tech way to consume cricket with the modernity of their cars, but the sum paid must still have been agreeably large for just one asset.

- Maruti for this fee ended up taking "most of the real estate" on the site, according to a report in: http://www.indiantelevision.com/mam/headlines/y2k7/feb/febmam88.htm
- The agency selling space on the site had then to change the structure of the remaining sponsorship packages from the previous presenting sponsor and four associate sponsors as there was now far less inventory available for other potential partners.

However, the biggest objection to title sponsorship is losing your own brand and identity behind that of the sponsor's name. Some events are sufficiently strong brands that they feel a title sponsor will devalue the equity built up in the name. Even for less established events, it is worth considering before entering the market that it might take away your ability to grow your property as a brand and your set of rights over time. Others may feel that the title sponsor will swamp the activity or dilute their ambitions with other sponsors.

This is being seen more and more, and below we show why one big golf event recently decided to drop title sponsors completely.

 Case Study: A national golf championship

 Key learning points:

- Previously had a Title Sponsor
- Looked at other prestigious events and decided to follow their policy of not giving away title
- Then put in a descriptive sponsorship structure – Proud Partner, Official Sponsor, and Official Supplier

Presenting sponsorship

- Another consideration in your planning is the idea of presenting sponsorship, a great strategy for keeping the equity in your own event name.

This is seen much more in the USA than in Europe but it is a very elegant solution for keeping your own event name. *The Indianapolis Tennis Championships Presented by Lilly* or *Dextro Energy Triathlon London Presented by Tata Steel* are good examples. In the first example, the event's name is first and the sponsor's name follows. The second manages to have both the title and presenting sponsor's name within the title.

Some properties have gone on to try to do far too much with the name when they have sold both the title and the presenting rights. This can lead to some rather ugly solutions which, in our view, lose value both for the sponsor and the rights-holder as in the examples below.

- Nissan UCI Mountain Bike World Cup Presented by Shimano
- Bridgestone Presents The Champ Car World Series Powered by Ford

 Key take-outs

- Look at yourself via the same lens through which sponsors view you.
- Lack of preparation is the greatest reason that your eventual sponsorship proposals may fail to sell.
- It is vital to carefully prepare an inventory of sponsorship assets – and then to segment them in order to protect sponsor rights from the top downwards.
- A valuation of assets builds confidence inside your organization and forms a good negotiating tool with sponsors.
- It is absolutely necessary to get the rights organized, and it is an advantage if this can be done at the preparation stage rather than later so avoiding a spaghetti of different and complex arrangements with different sponsors for different rights.

- Making the effort to really understand a sponsor's industry is the solution to offering personalized sponsorships without compromising the rights structure.
- Use descriptive names like Official Supplier rather than Gold, Silver, Bronze.

Summary

Pre-sales preparation is absolutely vital; those six hours spent sharpening the axe will bring immediate benefits for you. When talking to sponsors their main complaint is that people have simply not done their homework, and this applies before they have even contacted the sponsor.

The next chapter on *The Sales Process* shows that good preparation also pays off handsomely when the time comes to approach individual sponsors.

CHAPTER 8

THE SALES PROCESS

 ## Overview

This chapter builds on Chapter 7, which was about getting the foundations right before the selling process begins. Now it is time to learn about the sharp end of capturing a sponsor.

This chapter covers:

- Where modern sponsorship is today and what that means to you.
- Looking at the market, the very important area of research, and getting to know your sponsor.
- Working out who should be spoken to, and finding out more about them so we can have a successful approach.
- Getting in the frame of mind of looking at yourself from the sponsor's point of view.
- Five Questions Every Proposal Writer Should Ask. How to make sure your proposals stand out.
- Real life sales tips.

 ## Market realities

- Red Bull gets approached by more than 300 sports platforms per week.
- HSBC receives over 10,000 sponsorship requests each year. Only 25% of their sponsorship programmes are to do with media exposure and brand awareness. The majority 75% needs to demonstrate real business returns.

- Companies buy solutions not sponsorship.
- Your offering is simply a tool. Decision makers care only about the results they get from using it.
- The key to getting round all this is to really get to know your sponsor and do some proper research and homework.

A few comments from sponsors themselves:

> "We get inundated with opportunities.....People come to us and say "here's how much we want".... Nine times out of ten their pitch will fall on deaf ears. They haven't done their homework and are just out there selling their thing without taking the time to think how it might suit us."
>
> *Reproduced with permission of Tony Ponturo, VP of Global Media,*
> *Sports and Entertainment Marketing Anheuser-Busch*

A point made by a number of sponsors is that many sponsorship seekers are almost disrespectful by not talking to the brand or to that specific business. Another example is from Unilever, which summarizes the frustration that sponsors feel:

> "It really is very difficult to work with some rights-holders because they may know a lot about their own properties but don't seem to have made any effort to get to know about the brands they would like to work with."
>
> *Reproduced with permission of Michael Brockbank,*
> *VP Brand Communication Unilever*

Sales strategies: think sectors not companies

Although it is not perhaps instinctive, try to avoid thinking about individual companies as potential sponsors at this point and think first about sectors and individual industries. Figure 8.1 shows the main spenders in total reported value in 2009, and forms a useful starting point to illustrate the process.

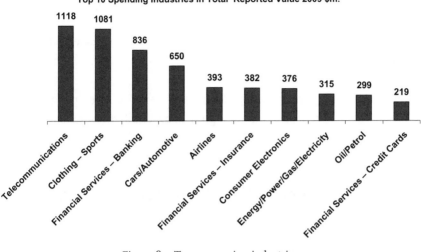

Figure 8.1 Top sponsoring industries
(Reproduced by permission of The World Sponsorship Monitor produced by IFM Sports Marketing Surveys)

If we take one of the traditionally biggest sponsors, say, car manufacturers, it can be seen that even though they were one of the industries most hit by recession, they still bought plenty of new sponsorship during that period.

The sales people at these events and other sponsorship properties making those sales, almost certainly knew what car manufacturers look for in sponsorship, and made sure that their proposals pushed as many as possible of their buttons or needs.

Car manufacturers' marketing needs

- They are always trying to find a way to get out of the showroom and meet up with consumers and customers almost face to face.
- They need to keep the loyalty of anyone who has already bought an expensive car from them. One way to do this is to be able to offer privileged access to desirable sports or arts events.
- They need to build the image of the brand or individual models, (sporty, refined, rugged, etc).

- They need to create something interesting that would appeal to would-be purchasers.
- Appearing at events can lead to test drives, views of new models, and stimulate dealers.

If an industry category is identified and considered to be suitable, and has some set marketing needs that we might be able to fill, the targeting can now be narrowed down to individual companies.

How research helps you to beat the market

We are often asked about the way to carry out some proper research on a sponsor. The list of required information in Table 8.1 is the basic minimum. With the power of the internet there is now no excuse for at least finding out about most of them.

It is necessary to find out what a company needs from its marketing to make sure that you will be addressing them in a relevant way. For example,

Table 8.1 Items of necessary information

Sales/Products *Marketing* *Geography*	It is now very easy to find out what a company does, where it sells it, and where they are based.
Company Reports	These are seldom used now because so much can be found online, but it is still useful and generally possible to download or ask for a free copy.
Google Alerts	This is an ideal way of tracking news on a company in which you are interested. It can be set up so that any news about it comes straight to your desktop in the morning.
Twitter and Facebook	Social media is another huge bonus for sponsorship seekers making information gathering so much easier than even a few years ago.
Press	Become an expert on the sector. There is plenty of specialist marketing or industry press for each individual sector. Sponsorship press like *Sponsorship News* or *The World Sponsorship Monitor* gives information on what companies are sponsoring and background on trends.

a new company that is in the first phase of existence in an immature market, as was the case for the telecoms sector 15 years ago, will need awareness. A few years ago it was the same with online gambling, as completely new brands needed exposure to encourage people to feel confident in placing bets with them. To satisfy these needs you would talk about gaining media coverage and exposure. For a company selling a product that is based on a very small business-to-business relationship, such as computer servers, then perhaps focusing on hospitality should be considered.

Who should I talk to?

At this point the real question is who to talk to, which is something we are frequently asked about. Before actually getting on the telephone and starting to make enquiries about contact names, the internet has facilitated this by listing contacts at companies (in most but not all cases). However, although the sponsorship manager will seldom be listed, brand managers are a good starting point. Another tip is to find the name and number of someone in the press department. Sometimes this appears at the bottom of a press release that has been posted online. Media relations people are often somewhat friendlier and more communicative than those in other departments and will often point you in the right direction. Once you have a name, you can visit sites such as Facebook and LinkedIn and so can start to get a good profile of the person you should be speaking to. This brings us to analysing the decision makers who are actually going to make the decision of whether or not to sponsor your property.

Decision maker analysis

How can more be found out about the decision makers in addition to information online?

- Personal contacts/mutual friends
- Industry gatherings/conferences
- Their other suppliers
- Talk to their colleagues, mention names

It is surprising how many people in your general circle will have contacts inside companies, so do use any possible means to try to find a way in. Suppliers are sometimes one way to find an entry point, but it is probably difficult to contact them out of the blue.

When it comes to making telephone contact we try to cheer up discouraged sponsorship sales people by reminding them that it can sometimes take six or seven telephone calls before you get through to the right person. However frustrating this may be, vital information can be picked up during the process of phoning. At this stage, visualize a network, or maybe even sketch a diagram, of who knows who and what the relationships are. If someone else in the company has already been spoken to, have that name ready in your notes to add to your credibility. All this preparation accumulates so that you can be truly ready to speak to the person you need to contact.

This may be fine, but at this stage people frequently become nervous about making a telephone contact and ask: "What should we do to get started?" Very few people like the idea of cold calling a company, and there is often a feeling that there must be someone out there with an address book full of the right contacts who could do this much better. However, although there are some specialist agencies, this is not always the case.

Cold calling

It is surprising, and quite encouraging, that some research from the USA by IEG shows that the majority of sponsorships have actually originated from a cold call (Figure 8.2).

Incidentally, some of the two biggest sponsorships in history of around $400 million and $750 million respectively (for Barclays and the New Jersey Nets' arena and Nextel and NASCAR) allegedly started with a cold call. One should not be afraid of picking up the telephone and starting out because it can be extremely successful, and given the fear people have of doing this you will stand out more than someone using an unsolicited email. While it is an advantage to be able to use any existing relationships such as advertising or specialist sponsorship agencies, there is really no short cut to getting on and starting on the long road towards getting your sponsorship sold.

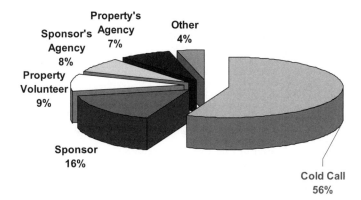

Figure 8.2 The importance of cold calling
(Reproduced with permission of IEG)

At this early stage of the sales process a lot really is all about your perception, and your efforts to try to understand the culture of the company. Make sure you listen rather than aggressively pitch. Try to feel, by what people are saying or not saying, how the company likes to do business. Doing this will allow you to:

- Tailor the style of the proposal
- Select the most relevant assets to offer
- Understand the real value of their offering to the target
- Identify who you should be talking to
- Be more effective at actually talking and communicating with a decision maker
- Develop the most persuasive messages.

During these talks it is reasonable for you to ask about:

- Past sponsorship experiences? (But make sure you have done your homework on this first!)
- Key issues – for their role, as well as for selecting a sponsorship property?

- How will they make the decision?
- Their motivations – Rational/Emotional/Political?
- Their current view of your property or activity?

The key thing is not to be too "salesy". Sponsorship is not going to be sold at this stage (unless you are very fortunate). A conversation about past sponsorships should yield much about how they feel about sponsorship. It is also an opportunity to show them that you have done your homework. Some tips from Carlsberg later in this chapter show how wasteful it is to approach a sponsor without having any idea of what it is they sponsor. It is unlikely that they will be spending money to echo something they already do.

Other areas to touch on include:

- What are the most important parts of sponsorship for them?
- What drives them?
- Why did they decide to engage in those sponsorships?
- How long does it take them to make a decision and how do they make it?
- Is it the Chairman's whim or have they developed some formal strategy when they put sponsorships through?

Previous chapters have looked at understanding your image, and learning about the context of how other people view your organization. Perhaps the company in question has some views or perceptions about you and what is being suggested that are completely at odds with the way you see yourself?

Also considered in this book is how, in sponsorship today, companies tend to pass the hat around different departments. It is likely that the person spoken to will eventually have to confer with colleagues in other departments, and you should cover how that is best done, and the arguments needed to help your contact to sell on to their colleagues.

A survey in 2006 tried to define the various different departments of companies involved in the planning and implementation of sponsorship (see Figure 8.3). In over half the cases it was public relations and advertising, as might be expected, but people are also involved who work in the direct sales and promotion departments. Your approach is going to have to appeal in some measure to all those people, with their different objectives and motivations.

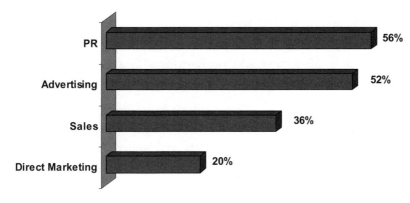

Figure 8.3 Sponsorship is integrated in the marketing mix. The 2006 Redmandarin European Sponsors Survey

(*Reproduced by permission of Redmandarin*)

Be topical: use trigger events

Things happen very fast in today's world and it is really a question of having the kind of mind that sees something happening and relays *useful* ideas or information to the potential sponsor. It could be a clipping or just a piece of information or insight, or a new product launch. It may be a difficulty that the company is experiencing, some general industry news, or some prominent new recruitment. Whatever it is, use these "trigger" events to be relevant and helpful. This is the time to try to find a "hook", or a connection with the company to show that you are following them, and that you might be able to actually help someone inside the company to perform their job more effectively.

Sponsorship is excellent at adapting to new circumstances and allowing creative sellers to make deals happen. A good example of what sponsorship should encompass is the swimmer Dara Torres, who won a silver medal in the Beijing Olympics at the age of 41. BP have a product called "Invigorate" which is designed to sustain the life of an old engine, but because of the recession consumers are not trading in their cars as early as previously and are trying to keep their old cars running for a few extra years. Torres became a spokesperson for Invigorate because someone very cleverly noticed the perfect fit. What you put in your engine can mean that you can keep performing at a very high level over a long period of time.

(?) Why write a proposal?

At some point in this process, after you have found the right person, will come the dreaded question:

"Can you put it in writing?"

This question can lead to fear and anxiety, and sometimes leads to a call to sponsorship consultants like us, because the idea of actually having to produce a written proposal is quite daunting for some people. In fact it is no bad thing as it forces you to consider:

- The need to systematically organize and list all of your assets
- The need to know the real value of all you have to offer
- The need to choose the most relevant assets for each company or product area and translate them into benefits.

The reason it is important to go through the process of organizing your materials is that in doing so you have to evaluate your assets, and organize them into a hierarchy that will make sense at a later stage to the sponsor. It also means that you have to think about what those assets are and how to translate them into benefits – and not merely make a list of features. After each point you put in writing you should ask yourself: "So what? What does that mean to the potential sponsor?"

- To support what sponsors like Carlsberg, Unilever and Budweiser say, some research done by Sponsorium at the end of 2009 found that the average sponsorship proposal meets just 44.8% of brands' needs.

(Reproduced by permission of Sponsorium)

We actually suspect that it may be even worse than that, which shows the quality of the materials people have to read and how easy it can be to get ahead of the competition by making sure that you are always relevant to the people you are speaking to.

? What should be written?

- *Proposal summary* – A maximum of 2 pages listing key facts and sponsor benefits.
- *Full proposal* – Includes covering letter, and supporting information. Detailed information for decision making and for sponsor to defend internally.

Proposal summary

The first action to take is to prepare a summary document, which should be short, one page only if possible. Follow this up with your full written proposal. At this stage people often ask if they should make a DVD or send something "a bit different". Good as it may be to have that type of thing and glossy brochures, most of them still end up sitting on sponsors' desks in a huge pile. It is not the format that is going to give you the cut through. It is your ideas.

Sponsors far too often see what are called "cookie cutter proposals" and they look something like this.

The property:	History, frequency, timeline
	Core values and attributes
Audience:	Size, demographics, TV viewership, purchase behaviour
	Levels of participation
The individuals:	Background, qualifications, experience, success
Other sponsors:	Rights, designations
Hygiene factors:	Ambush protection, security, insurance, risk management, weather, etc.
The offer:	Designations and logo usage
	Exposure opportunities on boards, internet, tickets, posters, venue
	Hospitality, personal appearances, database access, sampling, etc.

There is nothing wrong with this, in fact it is an excellent example. It describes exactly what the event is, how long it has been established, and how often it takes place. Sometimes these proposals talk about image and values, and sometimes not. They nearly always talk about media, sometimes in detail, and frequently rather vaguely or hopefully. Good examples show who you are and how the sponsor will be serviced, what you have done in the past and your experience of handling sponsors. Further detail of contingency plans, such as what will happen if the weather is bad, etc., would give even greater confidence in your professionalism. In nearly every case a proposal will talk about logo exposure, hospitality, tickets and other benefits.

This may all be absolutely fine, but *the problem is that it ignores the sponsor*. When thinking about big consumer companies like Gillette or Red Bull and the thousands of proposals they are having to process, we need to be totally personalized from the start, and this involves your covering letter or email.

Sending out 100 standard emails is absolutely counter-productive. To illustrate what sponsors have to face every day we have collected some examples of really bad first approaches:

TO WILLIAM,

"I would like to speak to someone, to see whether your company will be interested in sponsoring a music event that we will be running throughout the UK from this May. I have attached a PDF file that explains what this road show is all about and what benefits it may bring for your company. For more information, or if you have questions or queries, please do not hesitate to contact me ...."

Figure 8.4 Example of poor prospection email

Looking at Figure 8.4 the first warning sign is that this was sent to us, but we are not a sponsor; we are a sponsorship consulting business. Nevertheless, the person thought he would send it to us. The typefaces used are completely different, which tells me that it's been produced as a mass mail. *"I'd like to speak to someone, to see whether your company would you be interested in sponsoring a music event?"* This is an extreme example we agree, but there is absolutely no personalization, no research whatsoever. Also, sponsors will never be *"interested in sponsoring"*. Remember, they are not buying sponsorship; companies are buying solutions.

> *Dear Sir/madam*
>
> <u>*Please find the following attachments for your consideration*</u> *and assistance in obtaining sponsorship for our proposed event.*
>
> *Please don not hesitate to conatc me on 01234 56789 if you require any further assistance*
>
> *Kindest regards*

Figure 8.5 Example of poor prospection email

The second example (Figure 8.5) shows exactly how it appeared. "Dear Sir/madam", without even a capital letter on "madam", shows how little thought has gone into this. They have not even described what exactly it is they are offering, but have just attached a file which the prospect is supposed to open and have a look through. And then in the last line, there are even spelling mistakes, *"please don not hesitate to conatc me"*. It really is extreme, but the point is that there are too many of these emails out there irritating sponsors.

To be more positive, however, let us go through and look at some of the contents in setting out your basic summary which should be one page, most often used in an email:

- Totally personalized approach

The personalization comes from starting with an idea that is relevant to that particular company. *"I have a way for you to reach car owning college graduates who change their cars every three years."* Something like that gives impact, and shows that you have something that is worth reading rather than *"would you be interested in sponsoring a music festival?"*

- Lead with creative ideas relevant to that company, brand, service or product sector

The hardest and most important section of a proposal is to include one or two creative ideas, showing that you have thought about the potential sponsor and their business, and which will add considerable interest and stand out. A marketing person at Coca-Cola once told us he was looking for "something that adds colour to my day". If someone has gone to the effort of thinking up an idea, even if that idea will not work in reality, it still shows that you are the kind of person a sponsor could work with.

- Relevant audience information and profile
- What exactly is on offer

An exact and concise description of what is being offered should follow immediately, having talked about the audience for the sponsorship and the target group for the sponsor.

> "Everyone can prove reach, but is our audience passionate about this."

That point was backed by Rick Singer, Director of IBM Worldwide Sports Marketing (*Reproduced with permission of Rick Singer IBM*).

- Call for action

A call for action means ending a letter or email with a clear pathway of what will happen next, saying *"I will contact you if I may next Thursday"* rather than the awful phrase *"please do not hesitate to ask me"* used in the two letters above. If I were an interested sponsor, or wanted to find out more, believe me I would not hesitate.

The full proposal: basic structure and checklist

This document is to be used only *after* you have elicited interest and not in the early stages. Included should be the headings most people would agree should form a basic structure, and this section should be used as a checklist for your full proposals.

- Overview and event details
- Opportunity to reach target markets
- Media support and event promotion
- Creative ideas showing how the sponsorship will fit the sponsor's objectives
- Key rights
- Benefits
- Investment

The full proposal: overview and event details

- Key details on location, set-up of the organization or event. Details of team, individuals, history, background, event frequency, attendance, timeline, etc.
- Credentials, previous experience/events, previous sponsor handling.
- Clear expression of the image of the property, core values and attributes.

The overview and event details will be very similar to what has been used in the proposal summary but now is the moment to expand the description of the core of your offering.

The full proposal: opportunity to reach target markets

- What kind of people *exactly* do you bring to your sponsor?
- Overall popularity of the property, TV viewing, participation, attendance
- Detailed profile of fans' demographic, who are they, what do they buy, what do they do?

We have shown that sponsors really do like to see information on demographics, as underlined by Figure 8.6. When IEG asked sponsors in the USA "Which of the following characteristics do you typically analyse when making a decision to sponsor?" the answer was very clear.

If sponsors are asked about the key information they want to know when they make their decision to sponsor, they would like more than just informa-

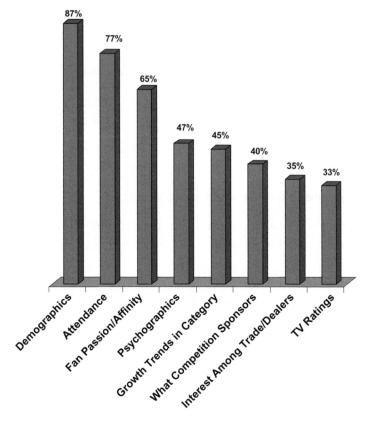

Figure 8.6 Importance of demographics to sponsors
(Reproduced with permission of IEG)

tion on whether your audience is male, female, age and so on. They want a feel for what kind of people they are and their behaviour. You must try to make almost a personal introduction to the fans of your activity. For example:

- Do they go on holidays abroad?
- Do they buy personal computers?
- Do they perhaps gamble online more than once a month?
- What is their propensity to purchase a sponsor's product or services?

Although it is often overlooked, this is very, very powerful information that should feature in a detailed proposal. For more about surveys and measuring sponsorship see Chapter 3.

The full proposal: media

- An accurate and convincing media plan
- Description of sponsor's exposure opportunities
- TV, press, internet, boards, tickets, posters, venue.

While most sponsorships in some way sell exposure and media, it is still very much hard currency in our business, and if it is going to be done well and described properly, it should be accurate. We see many proposals which say "we have a television station interested". While sponsors understand that media coverage is never certain until it is signed, it does look more professional at least to name the station, its coverage and audience reach.

The full proposal: key rights

- Who are the other sponsors?

In general the presence of other sponsors is an encouraging sign. They might also be sponsors who your potential sponsor feels would add prestige to their own presence, or they might like the idea of getting close to a co-sponsor who brings them business-to-business benefits.

- Is it cluttered with other sponsors?
- Event or category exclusivity?

Naturally if there are already plenty of other sponsors, perhaps they might consider that they may be going to get lost in the crowd and in the noise or "clutter". One way to reassure them on that point is to state clearly that you are able to protect them from sponsors competing in their own industry category by offering exclusivity.

- What are their rights, official sponsor, official supplier, signage, tickets?

Chapter 7 talked about how the use of descriptive names such as Partner, or Official Sponsor instead of Gold, Silver and Bronze helps to define more clearly the packages of rights for the various sponsors' levels. This is much easier for the sponsors to read and accept than having to compare a set of almost undifferentiated rights under Gold, Silver and Bronze.

The full proposal: examples of benefits

- Description of hospitality, meet and greet opportunities, VIP tickets
- Access and use of talent, team, venue or property.

If you are going to talk about hospitality, VIP packages and access to talent or other assets, it must be done properly and in detail. This should always be an attractive part of the proposal, harnessing the simple fact that most people in the sports, arts, charities, and public bodies engage in interesting activities with which people want to associate. Be very clear about what those benefits are and try to get people excited about them.

In Chapter 6, at the stage of organizing our assets, the following were discussed and they appear again below to add to your full proposal checklist.

- PR campaign tailored to sponsor's special interest
- Inclusion in all press releases and media activities
- Sampling to media
- Proposed advertising
- On ticket/event brochure promotions
- Use of your logos
- Availability of speakers for sponsor functions
- Access to mailing lists
- Opportunity to run database drawing promotion
- Business-to-business benefits
- Employee engagement/mentoring
- Product placement
- Merchandising rights
- Endorsement
- Provision of content for sponsor Internet site or social media

- Onsite sampling
- Use of property/venue for sponsors' events, customer relations, product launches, etc.
- Security, insurance, risk management, weather, etc.

The full proposal: do we deliver value and provide good service after the sale?

Not enough thought is given to making the sponsor confident in you and your ability to look after them.

- Who are the people that will actually be running the sponsorship?
- What are their credentials and do they have any experience?

Any company or individuals with experience in sponsorship know how incredibly time and resource consuming it is, and they will be concerned about the impact internally on frequently very-hard-pressed and sometimes overrun departments. They will ask themselves: What is the extra burden and cost going to mean?

You will be more successful if you can try to show that you have the means to take some of that burden away and work with the sponsor rather than just leaving it up to them.

This is also helpful later on because if sponsorships are not maintained, inertia tends to set in and, hence, they do not get renewed.

(?) Five questions every proposal writer should ask

Whatever items are decided for the proposal, it is important to step back, return to basics, and try to remind ourselves of what makes interesting and successful proposals. A good way of doing that is to ask the following five questions:

- Attention capturing?
- Highlight benefits not features – am I a business solution for them?
- Creative and proactive?

- Accurate and specific?
- Relevant?

Is this something that is really going to capture attention? Is it going to cut through the thousands of approaches made to a Red Bull or a Coca-Cola or a Carlsberg? Am I talking about myself or am I talking about the sponsor? Have I included something that is interesting and new and shows that I am thinking the right way? Is everything I have said totally accurate and not vague and woolly? And, most of all: Is this relevant? Is this something that is going to interest them?

Some sponsorship sales tips from Carlsberg

Carlsberg is one of the greatest consumer brands in the world and also one of the greatest sponsors with a huge portfolio of sponsorships ranging from the European football championships to music festivals and exhibitions. We can benefit from the direct advice of Gareth Roberts, who is their Director of Sponsorship and Media Relations:

- Do your homework.
- Make sure you know the history and current portfolio of sponsorship properties; don't try to "sell" something they already have.
- Accurate, up to date figures show a positive approach.
- Be clear up front on what it is you are proposing, do not generalize.
- Have a clear reason why it would fit, clear and accurate benefits.

continued on next page ...

- Don't attempt to put two things together that won't work, i.e. alcohol and boxing.
- Try to deliver the benefits at an early stage; the longer the pitch, the more likely a negative response.
- Try to get a strong reference from another sponsor.
- Even better, a reference from a current partner of the potential sponsor.

(Reproduced with permission of Carlsberg)

(?) "What is it you want?" Prepare your elevator pitch

At some point during this whole process you are going to be asked exactly what it is you want. Sometimes this may come slightly earlier than you expected. It might be after six or seven phone calls, or it might be on the first or second call. Therefore, do not blow your best chance by insufficient preparation. Having refined your offer down to the core, it is a good idea even to write it out.

When many people are asked that question they are put on the spot, and may say, "*Well, we are a tennis event and it's held every year and we have amateur players and professionals. ...*" That is perfectly accurate but it is not really going to help you to cut through, so what you should be doing is to say: "*We run a tennis event which allows us to offer car sponsors access to a young demographic who buy cars once every three years ...*" and then you have a conversation.

(?) Put the price in or leave it out? Involve the sponsor in the package

Another question often asked is whether the price should go in or be omitted from proposals, and this is a major point for discussion. Many sellers are unsure of the price they should be asking and in Chapter 7 it was shown how important it is to get this right. Those who have not gone through this process often give the event budget, hoping that the sponsor will somehow infer that the event needs X amount of money so the sponsorship fee must be Y. Perhaps they hope also that the sponsor has more experience than they do of sponsoring this type of activity, and will come back with a fair market value of what they should pay.

Talking about price early on saves time as sponsors live and breathe the budget they have this year and for following years. Therefore, if they have a broad idea of what they would have to pay for your sponsorship, this can only ease the decision-making process and save both sides valuable time. When it comes to the full proposal, the pricing should flow from the conversation about how the sponsor is going to get good value from what you are offering. Ideally both parties should arrive at a price jointly, while remaining flexible and negotiating around the benefits.

Sales tips for closing

- Invite them to the event
- Free sponsorship taster.

Perhaps one of the greatest assets people have when running events is that if the event is already in existence, you can bring potential sponsors in to experience it. During the recession we came across more instances of events offering to bring sponsors in for free for the first year. If they were given truly great service and managed to experience a real connection with fans of that event, the tactic should have a reasonable chance of going forwards on a paid basis for subsequent years.

- Use suppliers as sponsors

Another tactic which should perhaps be further considered is to turn first to your suppliers, with whom you already have a business relationship, to convert them into sponsors. For instance, areas such as signage, catering and printing could offer opportunities. Equally, insurance companies could provide a route for sponsorship that would ordinarily be overlooked. Most organizations have insurance and it is an industry that has quietly turned itself into a massive global sponsor as insurance companies look to buy some sort of personality for what is a rather dull, low involvement product. Go out and research your own insurance company; see if they are sponsors of anything else; calculate what you currently pay, plus any additional cover you might need for the future; and start the process by speaking to your existing contact within the company.

- Can you produce revenue?

Showing someone in a sponsoring company how they will be able to help to justify the sponsorship they bought if they can prove that it also generated revenue, is a powerful argument. It is not at all easy to link sponsorship to sales, but look for ways of doing this. This includes on-site sales, coupons, joint merchandising, store promotions or helping co-sponsors to do business together. We will discuss this further in the next chapter.

 ## Don't be passive: ask questions

When in the final stages it is important to ask key questions that will help you to reach your desired outcome:

- How long will it take to decide?

It is quite legitimate to say, "Well, we are talking now, how long does it generally take you to make a decision? How long does the process take?"

You must assume that the sale is going to happen and it would be reasonable to start talking about the new sponsorship in a collaborative way by asking if they have a standard contract, or if there is anything you can do to help them to make the signing happen more easily, or if there is anyone in the company that they would like you to talk to, for example.

- And if it's a no?...

Should you be facing the crushing disappointment of getting to a "no", make sure you realize (a) the lessons that can be learned from that, and (b) how you can build on it so that next time you can come back with a successful approach. Do not waste all that hard work.

"We have no budget"

Unfortunately this phrase is heard rather too frequently. It was heard often even pre-recession and has been encountered even more in the depths of the crisis. It is a comment that is provoked by a number of factors.

- It may in fact be true. There is an argument that if it is a really good idea, budget will always be found but, normally, unless it is a relatively small amount that can be found in a discretionary budget, many departments simply cannot find extra budget for the next twelve-month period. Sponsorship seekers often do not realize how far ahead companies plan and will ask for money just a few months from the event happening.
- The comment may also mean that you have been talking too much about your event rather than about the business results for them, and it is just a convenient blocking tactic. Go back and check that you have not just been talking features rather than benefits and have been relevant.

A practical way out of the budget problem is, say: "If you did not have to pay at all, would you then do it?" If the answer is "yes", try to work together to find a solution. For example, many in the recession were successful at adjusting the payments schedule, betting that sponsors would remain and would be in a stronger position to pay in succeeding years.

Other possibilities for defeating the budget objection include:

- Discounts for multi-year deals

The recession has dampened a positive trend where the sponsorship industry had understood that good sponsorship needs time to mature. Indeed, the first year of sponsorship is really a learning and benchmarking year. According to *The World Sponsorship Monitor* published by IFM Sports Marketing Surveys, the average duration of a sponsorship slipped from 3 to 2 years in 2009 at the height of the crisis and the pressure has been on to limit risk by signing shorter deals. It is therefore in your interest to keep and nurture the sponsor over a longer period, and so the revenue "given away" in the discount should be compensated for by an overall deeper relationship with that sponsor over time.

- Proportion of sponsorship fee payable up front

Your cash flow may be strong enough to allow you to help the sponsor over a budgeting hurdle by paying you the majority of the fee later in the life of the agreement.

- Share the risk

Chapter 7 looked at a trend, first seen in the USA, where the risk is shared or rewarded on the basis of delivering an agreed level of media or awareness shift for the company. This is not often done currently and it is a tactic that may, at least, agreeably surprise your potential sponsor and revive a flagging conversation.

☞ Key take-outs

- It is a crowded market.
- Companies buy solutions not sponsorship.
- Think Sectors – not Companies; look for the right buttons.
- Do your homework.
- Analyse the decision makers.
- Use trigger events.
- Ten totally personalized approaches are better than blanket bombing.
- Lead with creative ideas relevant to that company, brand, service or product sector.
- Talk benefits not features.
- Elevator pitch – don't just describe the event.
- Construct the price together, and be flexible and creative.

Summary

Companies do not buy sponsorship; they buy solutions to the business problems they face. Use this insight to stand out from the crowd and successfully attract sponsors. The next chapter shows how to keep and renew those hard-won sponsors.

CHAPTER 9

SERVICING AND RENEWAL

 ## Overview

The previous chapter showed that selling sponsorship is very difficult and is probably the hardest single area in this business. Therefore, to successfully retain a sponsor won through a great deal of hard work makes more sense than ever. That effort should not be wasted, resulting in having to repeat the cycle all over again. Successfully renewing sponsors is the Holy Grail of sponsorship sales and the ideal to work towards. The renewal process is an almost seamless extension of everything done from day one of signing the sponsorship, and that is the objective of this chapter. Good servicing not only helps you to retain your sponsors for longer, but can make lower level sponsors confident that if they move up to another level they will be well looked after.

This chapter covers:

- Fulfilling the sponsor after the sale, a continuous process which saves time and money and makes renewal easier.
- Remembering that sponsors are thinking almost from the start about whether the sponsorship is an appropriate activity or whether they could do something better with the money.
- Awareness. Be aware of the five questions every sponsor will ask themselves and will then be asking you.
- Under-promising, over-delivering.
- Continually reminding them why they are a sponsor.

Table 9.1 Different perspectives for sponsors and rights-holders

	Sponsor	Rights–holder
Business model	Shareholder imperative	"For the good of the game"
Accounting elements	P&L account	Cash flow
	Balance sheet	White knight
Performance measures	Share price	Winning
	Dividend	A full house
Human resources	Business Managers	Sports enthusiasts

Different perspectives

It must be recognized and accepted that the rights-holder and the sponsor will see things in different ways. More about this was explained in Chapter 2 but the motivations and working practices of both will never be the same. The only solution is good communication and the desire to understand the sponsor's perspective.

Table 9.1 indicates that if you look at both sides in the way you might look at a business, you find that what count as good outcomes are different and are measured entirely differently. What is striking is that sponsors measure performance in a much more quantitative, data-driven way than sponsorship rights-holders. This is worth remembering when you try to describe and report the beneficial effects you are generating for the sponsor. Marketing managers today are accustomed to seeing reams of data month by month on customer and competitor behaviour and live and die in a world of metrics.

Exploit sponsorship's flexibility in order to look after your sponsors

Sponsorship is a fantastically flexible marketing tool, which is why it has grown so strongly in the last few years. The point of Figure 9.1 is to show that once the sponsor has engaged and bought your property, there is a great deal that they can then do with it. It is very rare that a property comes up with suggestions and ideas for the sponsor, and even if nine out of ten of ideas are

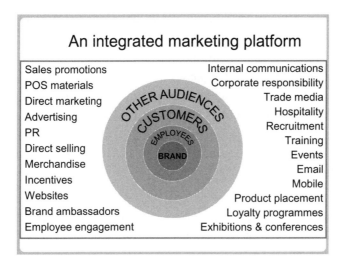

An integrated marketing platform

Sales promotions
POS materials
Direct marketing
Advertising
PR
Direct selling
Merchandise
Incentives
Websites
Brand ambassadors
Employee engagement

Internal communications
Corporate responsibility
Trade media
Hospitality
Recruitment
Training
Events
Email
Mobile
Product placement
Loyalty programmes
Exhibitions & conferences

OTHER AUDIENCES
CUSTOMERS
EMPLOYEES
BRAND

Figure 9.1 Sponsorship is an integrated marketing platform

not possible, sponsors very much appreciate the fact that their views have been considered and how they might develop their sponsorship.

Looking at Figure 9.1, the brand is placed right at the centre of the bull's eye quite deliberately because sponsors are mainly focused on what benefits are flowing to the brand from the sponsorship.

The sponsorship is capable of being exploited through many different channels and there follow some examples of suggestions that could be made to the sponsor if appropriate:

- Your sponsor must consider whether or not the sponsorship is having a beneficial effect on the company's employees. Do employees feel they are getting real benefits like tickets, or do they feel negative about a very expensive sponsorship when their salaries are under pressure?
- Is there anything more that could be done that would appeal to the sponsor's customers?
- Can help be given to advise the sponsor of other people who could be approached, such as investment analysts, government or NGOs?
- Can a brand ambassador be provided for a sports or cultural event?
- Can some website or social media content be provided?
- Can something topical for the sponsor's PR be provided?

- Is there a way some revenue could be generated through a sales promotion?
- Perhaps the sponsor has a new product or one under test where assistance could be given to help to sample it?
- Can a special event be created for hospitality in order to talk to prospects?
- Could some appealing content for competitions or database gathering exercises be created?
- Is the sponsorship helping make the company attractive to young students and future employees?

Remember: The job of rights-holders is to remind the sponsor of what else could be done with the sponsorship and remind them why they are sponsors.

How sponsors judge you

Your sponsor has usually been through a long process of strategy setting and planning before embarking on the actual sponsorship. Figure 9.2 is a typical illustration taken from a planning process for a real sponsor.

The initial three phases show the type of processes that sponsors may have been through even before they signed up for the sponsorship. It is not always so rigorous, but in most cases the process is generally much deeper than on the rights-holder side. What they will be doing, almost continuously, and certainly towards the latter part of the contracted sponsorship period, is looking at such questions as:

- Are targets being reached through this sponsorship?
- Could performance be improved?
- Are we, as sponsors, paying too much?
- Should we pay and do more to activate it, or is there a better alternative?

As previously referenced Figure 9.3 shows the key factors that sponsors think are important in a successful sponsorship from a survey undertaken by

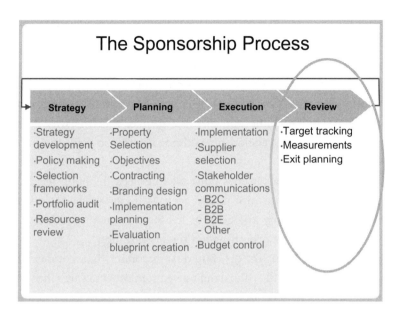

Figure 9.2 How sponsors judge you

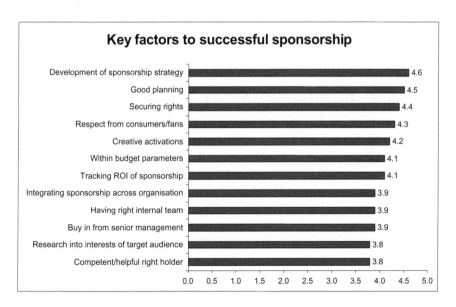

Figure 9.3 Key factors for sponsors
(Reproduced with permission of the European Sponsorship Association Survey 2007)

the European Sponsorship Association. Among the areas of particular importance on the rights-holder side is getting the right benefits package. The sponsors are also very concerned about whether the sponsorship is gaining respect from its fans or consumers. The rights-holders are the people responsible for bringing those fans and consumers to them, and the sponsor wants an authentic, genuine connection to those people, which is why it is very important to have a close relationship with the sponsor so that you can report back on this aspect.

Making sure the sponsor does not have to exceed the budgeted amount to make this sponsorship work is also seen as important because they, as individuals, have to justify and account for the investment and the budget they have secured and signed off within the organization.

Last on the list in Figure 9.3, but very important, is a competent and helpful rights-holder. As the whip hand moved somewhat towards the sponsor during the recession, sponsors are now, if anything, expecting even higher standards from rights-holders.

One of the parameters scoring 4.1 in Figure 9.3, and of great importance to the sponsor, is tracking the return on investment, and this is something that is worth looking into even more deeply because it is almost the key parameter for measuring sponsorship success.

Return on investment and return on objectives

The return on investment (ROI) and the return on objectives (ROO) are compared in Table 9.2.

Table 9.2 ROI v. ROO

Return on Investment	Return on Objectives
• Cash-based	• Variety of "currencies"
• Values outcomes in terms of financial efficiency	• Values outcomes in terms of how well objectives have been achieved

Return on investment

A simplification of ROI would be the sponsor working out what they paid you and then calculating how much they got back in terms of, perhaps, media exposure, awareness or sales. This is still very current in sponsorship but it is not a particularly satisfactory way for sponsors to measure, or for you to present, any findings that might persuade the sponsor to stay with you.

Return on objectives

Because sponsorship is so flexible it allows sponsors to try to make it meet distinct objectives. If you have carried out good research and performed quality pre-sale negotiations, you will have established an excellent partnership even before the sponsorship has started. You should also have a very specific idea of what they want to gain out of this sponsorship. If you can then measure according to what you know their objectives are, that will make the whole reporting – and ultimately the renewal – infinitely easier.

Measurement is without doubt a problem for sponsorship and sponsors complain regularly that the industry must work on a solution. Over the years various attempts have been made to find a common measurement standard much as in television advertising where Nielson supplies audience ratings and the entire industry agrees that a Nielson rating is the accepted unit. This is not the case in sponsorship and probably never will be as each sponsor is different, and they have widely differing objectives. Coca-Cola do not need to raise their awareness, but a new internet or mobile telephone or online gambling company certainly does; therefore, media exposure is less important for one group, while it is absolutely vital for the other.

Sponsorship Impact

We look in Table 9.3 at some of the things that can be measured that you should perhaps start considering when it comes to how you report value back to the sponsor.

Table 9.3 Sponsorship impact

Inputs	Amount of media coverage
	On-site exposure
	Likely audience exposed to property advertising
	Branded marketing materials produced and circulated
	Number of attendees
Outputs	Changes in attitudes to the brand
	Numbers signing up to a loyalty programme
	Improved B2B relationships
Outcomes	Improvements in customer purchase frequency and/or loyalty
	Sales achieved
	Commercial impacts of improved B2B relationships

SMART Objectives

Whatever measurement system is used, to get full benefit both for you and your sponsor try to test it against the SMART criteria:

- Specific
- Measurable
- Achievable
- Relevant
- Time bound

Five questions every sponsor should ask

This section is designed to give you the sponsor's eye view of you and to help prepare you to answer some of the very tough questions that sponsors ask themselves – and will consequently be asking you. These questions flow from the theory of how sponsorship works (Figure 9.4).

We will start at the top of the pyramid because the sponsor will always be looking at the benefit to the brand in terms of extra sales. It need not be restricted just to sales – other benefits can be planned, but the central focus will always be on how the sponsorship benefits the brand. Sponsors therefore

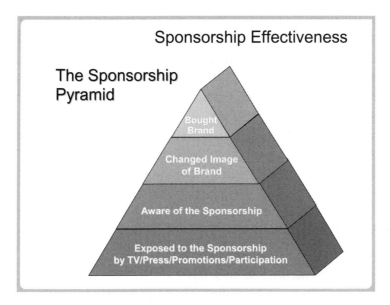

Figure 9.4 The sponsorship pyramid

are concentrating on the top of the pyramid, but most of them know that the process really starts at the bottom and works up.

Whether it is a local or community sponsorship, or whether it is the FIFA World Cup, it is always the same process. The way to have a happy and content sponsor is to expose as many people as possible to that sponsorship through TV, press, posters, flyers, etc., or online through a website or social media. Whatever the medium is, your job is to make that base as wide as possible. The reason for this is that elevating people from being exposed to sponsorship towards actually buying the brand is a very long, inefficient and difficult process. It is the hardest task in marketing to move people from just being exposed to the next stage up, which is to being aware. Even if they have seen something the question is, do they actually remember it? And if they remember that the sponsor was there, does that mean that they have any different perception of that particular brand, or that particular sponsor?

Changing people's perceptions of a brand is hard work, but harder still is making them change in such a way that they might actually select a different product when they go to the supermarket or a garage or online, when faced with almost identical brands. Sponsorship works mainly by increasing loyalty to a brand but it can also, when done well, shift perception enough to change attitudes and behaviour.

The whole process is almost intuitive to understand, but the problem is that it is also unbelievably inefficient, and as people move up the pyramid you are losing many of them at each stage. The job of the rights-holder, therefore, is to make the sides of the pyramid almost parallel so that you are not shedding hundreds, thousands or even millions of people at each stage.

Five questions every sponsor should ask

1. How visible was my sponsorship?
2. Did anyone notice the sponsorship?
3. Did it change perceptions of the brand?
4. How much more product did we sell as a result?
5. Should we renew the sponsorship?

Bearing the pyramid in Figure 9.4 in mind, the Five Questions Every Sponsor Should Ask will be: "Did I get good visibility, and if so did anyone remember me? And if anyone noticed or remembered me did this change their perception, and what did it do for us as a business?" The final and toughest question that really affects you is, "Is this something that we want to continue with?"

Q1. How visible was my sponsorship?

- Attendees

Attendance is quite easily measured and something you would expect as a given in any kind of reporting.

- TV/Press Exposure

TV/Press exposure is not particularly difficult, but it must be done properly, and care needs to be taken also how you present it. Sponsorship is not a cheap media-buying option to increase brand awareness. As discussed in Chapter 5 it is a terrible trap on the rights-holder side to present the sponsorship as being great value in terms of media exposure. There are some exceptions such as we showed in our case study of Ferrari and Vodafone in Chapter 1 but if a sponsor wants to buy media, generally speaking it would be much more cost effective simply to go out and do that from the many sources selling space. The best approach is to report the following, simply and accurately.

Quantitative: how much exposure the brand received

- Broadcast
- Print
- Web media
- Attendees

The quantitative side is actually quite straightforward and can be done yourself or by a specialist agency. Quantifying the value of all that media would be greatly appreciated by the sponsor, and obviously also useful for you in terms of renewing or talking to the sponsors later on.

Qualitative: the "quality" of the coverage received

- Brand involvement mentioned positively in editorial
- Communication of key messages with the piece

Instead of just receiving a cardboard box full of press clippings, which may be impressive for the first five seconds because you have had a lot of press coverage, the sponsor may ask: "Well, what do they say about us?" The rarity of getting a sponsor mentioned in the editorial, or a verbal mention on TV, makes it extremely valuable and an effort must be made to ensure that the sponsor is aware of it. Even better, and very much the ideal, is that one of the positive messages or attributes of the sponsorship or the sponsor has come through in the media. That is an excellent result if it can be proved to the sponsors.

Figure 9.5 High technology sponsor exposure measuring quantity of exposure
(Reproduced with permission of IFM Sports Marketing Surveys)

Exposure measurement

Measurement of television has moved on enormously and there are now many companies using image recognition technology, as seen in Figure 9.5, to measure sponsor exposure during sports broadcasts. Indeed some contracts stipulate a certain minimum amount of exposure, and third-party research companies provide timing reports on which large sums of money may depend.

Aside from measuring seconds of exposure, the IFM Sports Marketing Surveys' image recognition system, Magellan, allows insight into the visual impact of exposure by quantifying:

- Size
- Position on Screen
- Clutter
- Average Duration

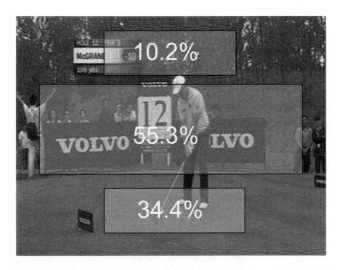

Figure 9.6 High technology sponsor exposure measurement measuring quality of exposure
(Reproduced with permission of IFM Sports Marketing Surveys)

As seen in Figure 9.6, the total visual impact defines how good the quality of a sponsor's exposures typically were. This takes the form of an overall factor (Visual Impact Score) whereby the closer to 100% the better the overall quality of exposure, on average.

The technology allows fast analysis of where exposure could be improved, as shown in Figure 9.7, and some events will even move and adjust boards during broadcasts, desperate to do a good job for their sponsors.

Thinking back to the pyramid in Figure 9.4, and widening the exposure base as much as possible, we encourage you to look at absolutely everything that will generate more visibility and exposure for your sponsor.

Other visibility channels

- *Sponsors:* Internal: email, intranet, magazines, canteen, notice boards, team meetings, reception areas

Source	Size	Position	Clutter	Av. Duration	Visual Impact Score
Caddy Bib	Medium	Good	Excellent	Medium	61.5%
Clothing	Low	Medium	Excellent	Low	33.8%
Clubhouse	Low	Good	Excellent	Excellent	56.3%
Course Flag	Excellent	Excellent	Excellent	Low	83.4%
Flag	Low	Good	Excellent	Low	23.9%
Interview Board	Excellent	Medium	Excellent	Excellent	93.3%
Panel - Driving Range	Low	Low	Excellent	Excellent	51.3%
Panel - Event	Medium	Medium	Excellent	Low	39.4%
Panel - Fairway	Low	Medium	Excellent	Excellent	26.6%
Panel - Green	Medium	Good	Excellent	Good	57.8%
Panel - Tee	Excellent	Excellent	Good	Excellent	95.7%
Panel - Water	Medium	Good	Excellent	Good	58.6%
Player Entrance	Excellent	Excellent	Excellent	Excellent	100.0%
PR Event Tee Panel	Medium	Excellent	Excellent	Low	59.7%
Scoreboard	Good	Medium	Excellent	Medium	70.8%
Screen Credit	Medium	Good	Excellent	Excellent	78.4%
Tee Marker	Low	Low	Good	Good	16.9%
Tee Number Board	Medium	Excellent	Good	Good	57.4%
Umbrella	Good	Good	Excellent	Good	91.5%
Winners Podium	Excellent	Good	Excellent	Low	68.1%

Figure 9.7 Fast analysis showing where exposure could be improved
(Reproduced with permission of IFM Sports Marketing Surveys)

- **Rights-holders:** advertising; ticket wallet; at event; magazine; audio-visual; online
- **Indirect:** the media; fanzines

Maximizing visibility means encouraging the sponsor to make sure that the event, the property and the relationship are publicized inside the company. Simple techniques can be used, such as providing updates on last weekend's event pinned on the notice board in the canteen, to company magazines, the intranet and email alerts. Perhaps an exhibit from an event that is being sponsored can be loaned to the reception area of the company so that everyone can enjoy it?

We once advised that a club which produced small-scale travel guides for fans travelling to games on buses made sure that their sponsor was represented there for the first time. All these things combined can add substantial extra value to the whole sponsorship, and importantly they also show that thought is being given to the sponsoring company, and the assets are being worked as hard as possible for them.

It has been shown how to make the bottom of the pyramid as wide and efficient as possible, but the next question that is going to be asked is "Did anyone notice this sponsorship?"

Q2. Did anyone notice the sponsorship?

Here we are measuring awareness, the vital middle step towards progressing or reinforcing feelings about the company or brand. Sponsors will ask themselves:

- What was awareness among my target markets?
- How much did it increase?
- How can I increase awareness?
- Have we reached a peak?

Table 9.4 summarizes what, in our opinion, are the main factors for driving awareness of a sponsor.

Measuring awareness

Figure 9.8 presents a real life example from the Olympic Games in Atlanta 1996. Coca-Cola has sponsored the Olympic Games since 1928, and Atlanta is their Head Office. Therefore it was very much "their" event.

When asking one thousand Americans by telephone in the months preceding the Games, the top brand awareness, as you might expect, was Coca-

Table 9.4 How can you help a sponsor to generate awareness?

Sponsor branding	• Obviously the amount of branding and visibility is very important; you cannot build awareness if you cannot see the sponsor.
Length of sponsor involvement	• Sponsorship is something that needs a long time to mature. It takes time for recognition to build up and a sponsor cannot expect within a year to achieve maximum awareness. In fact, year one is often just a benchmark year and we recommend to try and negotiate two or three year sponsorships.
Limited competitor activity/ ambush marketing	• Ensure that there is as little "clutter" as possible so that your sponsor can stand out.
	• Being able to offer sponsor exclusivity obviously helps in clearing the field for your sponsors.
	• While normally a problem for very large events, do make sure that you try to protect your sponsors from other companies stealing their thunder by passing off as an official sponsor of your event, which is called ambush marketing.
	• The best way to combat ambush marketing is to make sure that you and the sponsor are such a close and logical partnership that other companies just could not come over as being authentic and "right".
Extent of rights leverage	• This is the key issue for sponsors as they have to work as hard as they can to squeeze every drop of value out of any sponsorship. You must work as hard as possible by supplying creative ideas to do this and in executing the various leverage schemes to maximum benefit.
Synergy between sponsor and the activity	• Research shows that the most important factor for generating awareness is that there must be an obvious logical link between the sponsor company and the property. If people can feel intuitively that there is a synergy, then awareness will rise accordingly.

Cola, and that was named by nearly half of the respondents. However, a smaller, but significant, group thought that Pepsi was also an Olympic sponsor, which they were not, but because there is synergy there, and because of Coca-Cola's activities with the Olympics, people thought it likely that they were.

If we go to the two vertical lines in Figure 9.8, which is the period when the Games actually took place, Coca-Cola began to ramp up their promotional efforts and to leverage the sponsorship, and the awareness rises quite considerably. This forces Pepsi down and that sustains itself throughout the Games.

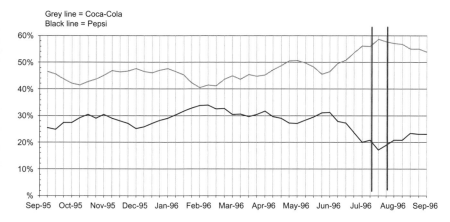

Figure 9.8 Tracking awareness around the 1996 Olympic Games.
Q. "Can you tell me any soft drinks that you associate with or believe sponsor the Summer Olympic Games?" (Source: SRi Sponsortest, reproduced with permission)

But looking at what happens afterwards, the awareness measures start to drop off because Coca-Cola cannot work the Games as hard and Pepsi's measure starts to rise. A few months later those two lines will be nearly the same again. This would be a good argument for Coca-Cola to renew in order to keep repeating the process and forcing the lines apart.

Awareness is important as part of the process but it is only part of the story in leading to changing perceptions of the brand.

Q3. Did it change perceptions of the brand?

This is more difficult to answer, but you can provide:

- spectator surveys
- verbatim comments
- guest feedback, etc.

As the rights-holder, one of the best things you can do, but which is often overlooked, is to exploit your ownership of the event or activity to survey people and to find out more about their perceptions of the sponsor. Not only that, but you can add questions such as: "What kind of sponsor would you expect to find at this event?" (Which is very useful ammunition for future sales.)

It is also very powerful when reporting to a sponsor if you give some quotes or verbatim comments from either spectators or hospitality guests who have enjoyed the experience and have had a positive association with the sponsor.

The importance of market research

While some sponsors do research their sponsorships, others frequently do not. According to an ANA/IEG Survey in 2010, only 35% of respondents "always or almost always" measure their sponsorship and event marketing activities' returns. Sometimes they rely on word of mouth, anecdotal, feedback from dealers, water cooler conversations, feelings around the company, and so any research that you can supply is likely to give them a more fact-based platform than just perceptions. You can always offer access to event/spectator research for extra industry-specific questions. For example, if you have a car sponsor and you can tell them how many of your fans bought a car in the last 12 months, and their awareness of the brand in question, it is beneficial for the sales process and shows you are thinking in the right way.

Q4. How much more product did we sell as a result?

The fourth question is very hard for you, the rights-holder, to answer:

- You cannot measure their sales, but always try to generate some level of revenue ideas for the sponsor.

For example, for a telephone company, SMS votes have a potential for gaining some revenue, and can help to soften the budget. Posing an idea like that is positioning you as a business partner rather than just the recipient of money.

It is not always as crude as "did we sell more product?", and, as we have seen, there are other objectives that companies have apart from straight sales.

However, as this is the most typical objective it should be looked at more closely.

- Did orders/distribution to guests increase?
- Was coupon redemption above average?
- How much product was sampled?

It is a problem for sponsors to isolate sponsorship activity and sales activity and try to link them because competitors change, the sponsor and their competitors run advertising or promotional campaigns, and there are also natural cycles in a sales year. It is very hard for the sponsor to say definitively "our sales rose X%" over the time of the sponsorship. But it can be done with things like tracking orders from any guests or event-linked coupons or an event-linked on-pack promotion, and sponsors in the USA do this more often than other parts of the world, as can be seen in the case study below.

 Case Study: Sponsored food on Horizon Air

 Key learning point:

- Measuring response generated by a sponsorship is occasionally possible and sometimes can be very precise using social media.

In May 2010 passengers on Horizon Air flight 2631 from Seattle to Portland were handed out sponsored boxes of food under the AirAdvertainment free lunch/snack programme. The box contents included Stacy's Pita Chips and Hershey's chocolate, and was sponsored by Creative Labs, which used the new medium to promote a Facebook contest to name its Vado HD 3rd generation video camera. The box design featured a "call to action" for the contest and 25,000 boxes were distributed to Horizon Air passengers over 20 days. "With

continued on next page ...

certain airlines cutting services and adding charges, this program is a welcome addition for passengers and operators alike," said Mary L. Macesich, co-founder and Vice President of AirAdvertainment. "Passengers are thrilled to receive a snack or bite to eat, the airlines are excited to be able to provide it at no cost, and the brand finally has the ability to connect with the public in a captive environment where they are spending time, largely undistracted. All with a social media kick."

(Reproduced by permission of AirAdvertainment)

One sponsor a few years ago was very impressed when they put a NASCAR racing car outside a big supermarket. To sit inside the show car and meet the driver you actually had to purchase the sponsor's goods inside the supermarket and collect a coupon. For some diehard redneck males it was allegedly quite literally the first time they had ever been in a supermarket! That is trackable, it is impressive, and it illustrates the power of sponsorship.

Because access to a company's sales figures is not usually available, some creative rights-holders have attempted to link movements in a company's share price with the sponsorship. While sponsorship is just one small factor having an influence, the fact that you have taken the time and trouble to do that would show that you are someone a sponsor can work with, rather than just a passive money taker.

Q5. Should we renew the sponsorship?

This final question is going to have a huge influence on your professional lives as rights-holders. Sponsors will always be saying to themselves:

- Has it worked?
- Can it work?
- How much should we pay?
- Is there a better alternative?

In this very tough world where there is always a risk of losing your sponsor, or of them trying to renew at a discount, you must help the sponsor to answer these questions. Below are some tips to help you to retain them.

Tips for servicing a sponsor

Develop a common understanding

It is a relationship and, like any other, it helps if you can agree on the ground rules, and the vocabulary and medium of the relationship.

- The sponsored activity:
  - scope
  - rules
  - vocabulary
  - key players
  - industry standards

- The business arrangement:
  - partnership objectives
  - contractual obligations
  - company jargon
  - organization structure
  - key contacts

Importance of measurement and servicing

- Give sponsors relevant information, ask what they need – e.g. a B2B does not always need press cuttings.
- Keep a continuous sponsor activity log.

Instead of just sending a report with a photograph of the event with a sponsor's logo visible on a board, make sure that every meeting, every telephone conversation, every idea that you have suggested, every single outcome of the sponsorship has been recorded and logged. Later on you can edit it and show just how much extra value you have given because these regular small actions are very quickly forgotten by both sides.

- Detail any extra activity and/or over delivery.
- Be accurate and realistic.

This is not a time to be modest, but nor is it a time to be inaccurate, so be accurate and realistic; but if you have done something more than originally promised, make sure the sponsor knows about it.

- Present it in person and talk about issues, future upgrades and renewals.

Have the courtesy of going to present that report in person, or at least offering to come and present it. Tell them you have ideas, and you want to discuss how things could be improved and how weak areas could be addressed.

- Talk about renewal before they do.

Raise the subject and make it into a dialogue rather than just having them sending you a letter six months before the end of the sponsorship informing you that it is all over.

Create extra value for your sponsors

Other suggestions that rights-holders are trying at the moment include:

- Create a Sponsors-Only password-protected website, or an area on your website, to store fulfilment reports, event info and research.
- Organize sponsor workshops.

According to IEG, only 50% of properties organize workshops but it is a good idea to get your sponsors together and see if you can help them get more out of your property, one way being to help them to see if there is any business they can do with each other. A workshop could make them feel that they have a mouthpiece, and allow them to get rid of any gripes, and address issues during the sponsorship rather than during the period when they are perhaps thinking about whether or not to renew it.

- Invite prospects.
- Give relevant news, audience research and new sponsorship opportunities.
- Educate partners about their co-sponsors.

A word of warning, however, about sponsor workshops. If you have not defended your set of rights and prices as we suggested in Chapter 7 your spaghetti of different deals can unravel if your sponsors start talking to each other and you do not have a rationale for those prices and rights.

The other thing to be aware of when considering a workshop is to be sensitive and marketing savvy enough to know that different sponsors can have totally different objectives, so one size will not fit all. Some sponsors care about service endorsement, some hospitality, some top of mind awareness, some B2B and some brand image or media coverage.

More ideas to keep sponsors happy

- Create a 5% of fee activation budget.

This has been tried occasionally in America, but much less so in Europe. You could suggest that from the amount of the money you receive in exchange for the rights, you will apportion a certain percentage to activation and making the sponsorship work harder on behalf of the sponsor. We have seen this ratio as high as 15%, but that could be too high and would deprive you of much needed income, even if in any case you would be spending at least some budget on sponsor activation. If we calculate at 5% on the value of most sponsorships, you generally find there is enough money to pay for some good PR, special mail outs or other promotions, some side events or even a modest amount of paid advertising. The idea that a guaranteed proportion of their money is going to be used to help to activate the sponsorship is generally welcomed by sponsors and in any case it is a different approach that helps to set you apart from the crowd.

- Suggest new ideas regularly, use "trigger" events.
- Do not let them forget the reason for being a sponsor.

Sponsorship staff inside companies are extremely busy, often overwhelmed, and they will appreciate it if you can do some of their thinking for them. For example, you might suggest a new speaker or appearance, a new use of a venue, or a Tweet or some content for a forthcoming company event. Try to keep your ideas topical, relevant and fresh.

- Tie in cause/community relations efforts.
- Provide "ownable" platforms. Provide something that the sponsor can put its name on within the event, something that no other sponsor can associate with, an online or social media action or an event lounge for example.
- Be flexible when a sponsor experiences change.
- Offer new inventory and other support elements.

 ## Key take-outs

- Servicing a sponsorship is something that should happen from the beginning – it should not be something that happens in a panic towards the end of the sponsorship period. It is a continuous process to make sure that the renewal is always kept uppermost in mind, and that nothing is forgotten.
- Remind them of why they chose to be a sponsor, make sure that you add value as you said you would, and make sure that you have proven it with data.
- One key to keeping a sponsor is that sponsorship is a very flexible medium that works on a brand, customer and employee level. Remind them of all the many different ways they can use this sponsorship; do their work for them, and help them to get real value from it.
- For better or for worse, return on investment is still important in the sponsorship world. It is a fact of life, so measuring returns needs to be carried

out properly and you can assist with that. Chiefly, however, it is moving towards return on objectives, and so you must learn your sponsor's objectives at the outset. Helping the sponsor's employees to report on the key things that are of concern to them helps them keep their jobs and get their pay rises. You will get a nice warm glow from your sponsor if you can do that for them properly and professionally.

- Visibility is just the start as we move up that pyramid, but remember to make sure that you have made the bottom layer as wide as possible so that sponsors can gain the visibility that leads to awareness.
- Use the power of knowing who your fans are, and be able to drill down deeply and use their enthusiasm for the property to provide valuable insights for the sponsor.
- Try to suggest how the sponsor can make some money to help to defray the cost of the sponsorship, perhaps through combining business with another sponsor, or having a joint promotion.
- Always keeps a log containing every single element of the activity. It is a good record and it will make producing your sponsor report much easier.
- But most of all be alert. The world is changing faster and faster; that presents threats, but also opportunities. The good old days when football clubs used to say "a good sponsor is one we don't hear from until it's time to renew", have completely gone. So without being on the telephone to your sponsor every moment of the day, you do need to show that you are sensitive and aware and are looking for opportunities not only to help them, but also to help them to do their job.

Summary

The key to retaining sponsors is effective servicing from the moment a sponsorship contract is agreed. Understanding sponsors' objectives, assisting them in achieving their aims and, crucially, reporting on activity and successes regularly will all play a part in sustaining effective sponsor relationships over the long term.

Part III
The Way Ahead

CHAPTER 10

SPONSORSHIP IN THE FUTURE

 Overview

To wrap up *The Sponsorship Handbook* this final chapter summarizes the main trends affecting the sponsorship industry over the next decade. We make some predications on where these trends are likely to take us and what they might mean to those of us in the industry, whether sponsors or rights-holders.

This chapter covers:

- The impact of the recent recession.
- Trends already under way across:
  - The industry in general
  - Sponsors
  - Rights-holders

Impact of the recession

As much of the world struggles to regain momentum in the wake of the recession, its impact on sponsorship cannot be ignored. In the short term, at least, there are two immediately recognizable impacts: risk aversion and lack of funds.

Risk aversion

It is noticeable that there have been fewer new organizations investing in sponsorship. This is mostly due to the relatively high risk nature of sponsorship. Organizations that were sufficiently risk averse not to have already included sponsorship as part of the marketing mix prior to the economic downturn are unlikely to embrace it while there is any question over the future.

The other noticeable impact of recession-related risk aversion is that average sponsorship contract terms are reducing from around three years to two years. This is being driven by both sides of the sponsorship relationship. Sponsors do not want to be tied in to long-term relationships when they are unsure of the economic upturn. Equally, rights-holders – many of whom have had to accept lower prices for their properties in the short term – want the earliest possible opportunity to re-sell rights at a higher price on the assumption that the rights market will recover.

Lack of funds

As already alluded to, the sponsorship community has not remained immune to the recession. Rights-holders in particular, whose businesses would always be perceived as higher risk by the nature of their operations, have found it particularly difficult to secure bank funding. Equally, those rights-holders that have historically relied on government funding have been under no illusion that the status quo will remain.

This has made sponsorship as a source of funds even more important to rights-holders. Consequently, they have been much more willing to negotiate lower fees and shorter terms to ensure that sponsorship monies continue to flow, rather than retain the perceived high value for their properties established pre-recession but for which there is no current market.

Sponsors have also had to significantly trim their budgets and, with less to spend, this has contributed to the downward pressure on sponsorship fees. As another consequence, this has led to greater competition for the higher value properties, resulting in increasing polarization between the fees secured by the biggest rights-holders compared with smaller properties.

A catalyst for change

However, the recession has also had a positive impact on the development of sponsorship globally, acting as a catalyst to accelerate trends already under way, including the creation of more genuine partnerships between sponsors and rights-holders and a greater focus on authentic activation.

Partnership development

While it is still alive, like Chairman's whim sponsorships, the "cash and dash" type of sponsorship arrangement – where a sponsor signs the cheque, organizes some branding and enjoys the hospitality but does little else to activate the investment – is on the wane. Sponsors and rights-holders are both recognizing the benefits of working more closely together to understand each others key drivers and identify ways in which they can contribute to mutual success.

This has resulted in greater goal sharing and even alignment, supported by increased interest in performance-related pay. This is where the rights-holder earns part of the sponsorship fee as a bonus for assisting the sponsor in achieving their sponsorship objectives. Some examples of this might be:

- A lump sum bonus for achieving a certain number or percentage of sponsor mentions in the media as a result of the property's own PR efforts.
- Stepped payments when the sponsor achieves certain targets in advance of what they would expect, based on the rights-holder's extra branding efforts.
- A payment per record relating to the success of a database generating scheme from among property fans by the sponsor.

This trend also manifests itself in the increased use of value in kind and marketing in kind as part of the sponsor's contribution to the relationship. From a rights-holder's perspective, budget-relieving benefits in kind all assist in managing cash flow. For sponsors, the provision of benefits in kind contributes to their being a credible, and therefore more acceptable, partner to the property in the eyes of its fans.

Authentic activation

While there is undoubtedly still a lot of room for improvement, there is definitely a greater appreciation by sponsors of their role in activating a sponsorship to generate returns. Sponsors are becoming more creative in their activation programmes and in particular are increasingly:

- Recognizing that they are effectively an uninvited guest at the fans' 'party'. As such, sponsors need to proactively make a contribution to the fans' experience, the equivalent of 'bringing a bottle'. To be authentic, this will in some way reflect the sponsor, its products and services and the messages they are aiming to communicate.
- Using the power of social media to amplify leverage of purchased rights such as athletes and unique content. Social media also has the advantage of being a very efficient investment. It allows easy access to very defined groups, such as fans of a personality or an event through Twitter or Facebook, for example. Sports fans especially are always data- and news-hungry and sponsors who are felt to help in providing information and insights to fans will gain goodwill.

The ability to segment and measure these digital communities is an extremely welcome addition to the world of sponsorship, which will only assist in fuelling its growth. Sponsors will also learn so much more about how fans feel about them and the level of possible engagement than was ever possible before.

The challenge which brands face with social media is that the 'rules of engagement' differ widely from traditional mass-marketing channels. This creates two distinct challenges:

- *Tone of voice:* Rather than a one-way channel, social media is a dialogue where all users have the same rights to create and shape the content. Overt commercialization is not part of the new online etiquette and the successful sponsors of the future will be those who are seen to be taking the right tone when joining in the conversation.
- *Loss of control:* Organizations across the marketing spectrum are struggling to accept that they are no longer totally in control of promoting their own

brand. Get it wrong and you will be virally vilified around the world in seconds. Get it right and you enhance brand perceptions, loyalty and positively impact the bottom line. Those sponsors and rights-holders that are brave enough to reach out and invite social media activists to the party will reap the rewards.

The trend of investing in grassroots or associated corporate responsibility activity as a way of getting closer to fans and demonstrating a sponsor's commitment to the sponsored property is also seeing significant growth.

Ultimately there is recognition that fans will largely no longer tolerate sponsors who are not perceived as making a valid contribution to enhancing the sponsored activity in some way. Sponsors are rising to the challenge to ensure that their participation is valid, noted and, progressively, valued by fans.

Industry development

Sponsorship is a lag indicator in recessionary times and therefore it is expected that it may take longer to recover than other sectors of the economy. In the case of sponsorship, this means that it will continue to grow, albeit at a slower pace than the last decade, primarily at the expense of traditional advertising.

One result of the digital revolution is the need to draft a new definition of sponsorship. This will take account of developments in digital media, and especially social media, and the opportunities this presents for new business models to be created that can successfully command sponsorship investment as channels to particular target audiences.

The numbers looking for sponsorship will increase as governments universally cut public spending while they pay back debt. Those that have historically relied on government funding, largely in the cultural sector, will now have to gear up to attract commercial sponsors. This is not without issue, as these organizations wrestle with the challenge of commercial involvement and 'editorial control', whether that is curatorial or artistic direction. Equally, they will fail to attract sponsors if they are not able to demonstrate a coherent and well-organized structure that is specifically tasked at looking after sponsors' interests.

As mobile telecoms develops as a communications channel, rights-holders and sponsors will both look to leverage this highly personal medium to engage consumers more deeply with their properties and sponsorships.

Permission-based marketing will eventually create a much richer experience for consumers but it will take time, and some false starts, for all parties to understand the parameters of acceptability such that this channel is really able to deliver a win–win–win.

New rights-holders with a willingness to work in tandem with a sponsor will attract interest because they offer sponsors the opportunity to develop something fresh without the risks of creating a wholly owned activity.

Sponsors

As sponsorship gains stature within the marketing mix, based on its ability to provide a platform for two-way engagement with customers and other stakeholders, companies will increasingly insist on robust strategies to inform their sponsorship activities. While this will not totally ring the death knell for Chairman's whim sponsorships, it does suggest a significant reining in on off-strategy sponsorships.

With a better understanding of how sponsorship works and its inclusion in the marketing mainstream, it will benefit from being exposed to, and integrated with, the planning tools and techniques operated by other marketing disciplines. This will not only improve implementation planning but will also promote a greater appreciation of the financing of sponsorship activation. After all, nobody expects to invest in creating a 30-second TV advertisement without having allocated the budget for buying the media in which it will be shown.

Attracting and retaining consumers' attention will become progressively harder and will be met with a wave of creativity as brands try to gain a cut through with their sponsorship activities. While there will still be sponsorships where the objectives call for little more than brand exposure and/or hospitality, the cost-effectiveness, flexibility and reach of the digital sphere and the need to create engaging brand experiences will lead to a more holistic approach to leveraging sponsorship rights. This, in turn, will drive up returns from sponsorship, which then increase sponsorship's perceived value to the sponsor's organization, which will open the door to further investments, creating a virtuous circle that will contribute to the ongoing growth of sponsorship globally.

An increasing appreciation of sponsorship is resulting in it taking on a more strategic role for sponsor organizations. Objectives are being more carefully crafted with reporting performance in mind and it is inevitable that the research industry will continue to develop new tools and techniques to satisfy the increased need for relevant measurement methodologies. Equally we anticipate seeing greater investment in econometric modeling as sponsors look more closely at the relative value delivered per dollar spent across the marketing mix.

Rights-holders

Robust sponsorship strategies lead to more successful sales, happier sponsors and saving money and time renewing those sponsors. Rights-holders will benefit by working in an increasingly harmonious environment that is more supportive of sponsorship. The clear understanding of the objectives of each sponsorship relationship, and the accrued benefits, will insure the commercial team against internal stresses both in the short and long term.

Sponsorship sales will no longer be viewed as a numbers game. With competition for sponsors' money increasing, and a greater understanding and sophistication of sponsorship within companies, thorough preparation prior to going to market will become more common. Significantly fewer companies will be targeted, but the conversion rate will increase exponentially. Tailoring rights to fit sponsor needs will become the norm.

Those selling sponsorship will see ever greater pressure to demonstrate how sponsorship will deliver benefits to the sponsor. This will require rights-holders to think broadly about the variety of sponsors' objectives on which they might deliver and how to implement simple but effective measurement methodologies that articulate their contribution to a sponsor's success. Calls for ways of measuring sponsorship are heard ever louder from sponsors, and rights-holders who offer good-quality reporting systems will benefit.

Understanding the business problems of companies will get harder as the pace of innovation spawns whole new industries and companies, such as Google and Facebook, which rise from nowhere very rapidly. Sponsorship sellers will need to become much more expert at tracking and predicting these changes and understanding fast-moving hi-tech businesses if they want to be real partners.

Summary

As the industry matures, sponsorship will continue to grow and increasingly form an essential element in most organizations' marketing mix. The paradigm will shift to create an appreciation that sponsorship is:

- A marketing platform that can be integrated into all other elements of the marketing mix.
- Interchangeable with other creative solutions, rather than merely one possible route to market.
- A triple win partnership between sponsor, rights-holder and fans.

Greater professionalism in management and creativity in execution will be reflected in the respect shown to all parties that come together to create powerful sponsorship outcomes. This young marketing discipline has so much to offer and organizations will work hard to optimize returns over time. We are excited by the stimulus given to sponsorship by the emergence of strong industries and brands in Brazil, China, Russia and elsewhere and the speed of innovation in IT and in social media. All these factors will drive sponsorship forward ever faster and we hope this book will be a part of building competence and confidence in using sponsorship as a powerful and flexible marketing tool.

For further inspiration and ideas visit http://www.sponsorshipstore.com, follow us on Twitter as Sponsorshiptips or sign up for our regular Market Insights report at http://www.sponsorshipconsulting.co.uk.

GLOSSARY

Activation: The process of bringing a sponsorship to life through transforming the rights acquired into meaningful benefits that assist a company in achieving its sponsorship objectives, e.g. transforming the right to a certain number of tickets with corporate hospitality into a consumer competition and/or a high end business entertaining opportunity. Sometimes known as sponsorship exploitation or leveraging.

Ambush marketing: Any activity carried out by a brand that is not an official sponsor (often sponsors' competitors) of a particular property with the intention of gaining commercial advantage by establishing an association with the property in consumers' minds.

Assessment: The process of assessing the suitability of any potential sponsorship property against the business and marketing objectives of a specific brand.

Assets: The elements sold as part of a sponsorship, also known as sponsorship benefits. These may be tangible, e.g. perimeter branding, hospitality tickets, or intangible, such as the right of association.

Awareness: Used as a measure to establish that the target audience associates a sponsor's brand with the sponsored property.

Benefits: Advantages offered to a sponsor by a rights-holder as a result of the sponsorship assets acquired, e.g. if the asset is on-site signage, the benefit is the impact on spectators.

Brand tracker: A regular survey carried out into the health of a brand among its key target audience(s) that measures brand affinity, advocacy, brand attributes, usage and attitudes.

Consideration: The legal term that encompasses what the sponsor provides in return for the sponsorship rights and assets it acquires from a rights-holder, which may be one or more of money, marketing in kind or value in kind.

Evaluation: The process of establishing whether a sponsorship has achieved the objectives ascribed to it at the outset. This includes both measurement and interpretation of outcomes.

Exploitation: An alternative, and now considered old-fashioned, way of referring to sponsorship activation the programme of activities that a sponsor develops around the rights purchased to bring a sponsorship to life.

Fees: The amount paid by a sponsor in exchange for access to certain agreed direct and indirect benefits, the most notable being the right to publicize an association with the sponsored property.

Intangible assets: Elements of a sponsorship where there is no direct or associable cost, but that nevertheless have a value to the sponsor, such as goodwill.

Intermediary: Any third party that acts to facilitate the sale or purchase of a sponsorship, e.g. sales agencies, sponsorship consultancies, lawyers.

Inventory: The advantages offered to a sponsor by a rights-holder, often used in relation to those things that are in limited supply and therefore need proactive management, e.g. event tickets, hospitality passes, event programmes, hotel rooms, branded merchandise, etc.

KPI (Key Performance Indicator): Those measures that have been identified as the key to establishing how the sponsorship is performing in terms of achieving the sponsor's and/or rights-holder's objectives.

Leveraging: An alternative way of referring to sponsorship activation, the process by which sponsors develop programmes around the rights they have purchased to bring their sponsorships to life for their target audiences.

Market/consumer research: The process of understanding to what degree (quantitative) and why (qualitative) consumers react in certain ways. Traditionally, data is gathered by questionnaire or from focus groups and then analysed.

Marketing in Kind (MIK): Where a sponsor uses its own marketing reach to amplify the marketing efforts of the sponsored property to increase awareness and interest in the property and so drive, e.g. property ticket sales, property database registrations or influencers' opinions.

Media research: The process of understanding media exposure for a sponsorship and equating it to the cost of advertising.

Media value equivalence: A figure derived from adding together the number of minutes or column inches in which a sponsor's brand is exposed in TV coverage or print media, and then calculating how much this level of exposure would have cost for advertising in that medium. This figure is often then discounted by a percentage (known as the discount rate) in recognition that advertising allows communication of key messages that are not present in this activity-related media coverage.

NPD (New Product Development): The process of undertaking research to identify potential new products or services, then developing that research into a commercially saleable product or services.

Official Supplier: These are sponsors that provide budget-relieving value in kind to enhance a sponsored activity (and sometimes make an additional cash contribution as well) in return for being able to create an association with the sponsored property by marketing themselves as an Official Supplier.

Presenting Sponsor: A term used to define either the main sponsor, or the second most important sponsor behind a Title Sponsor of a property. The designation is normally constructed as "Title Sponsor Name (if there is one) Property Name presented by Sponsor Name", so maintaining a degree of separation between the Presenting Sponsor and the property.

Property: A project, event, team, venue or other entity offered on the market for sponsorship, usually but not exclusively from the sports, cultural, entertainment, charity or grassroots sectors, e.g. a specific art exhibition, a music festival or a sports team.

Qualitative research: Provides contextual information through focus groups, interviews.

Quantitative research: Provides statistical information based on a sufficiently large sample of people to be considered representative of the audience. Usually involves the completion of a questionnaire on paper, by phone or online.

Rights-holder: The person or organization that owns the physical or intellectual rights to the sponsorship property, e.g. Tate Modern or FIFA.

Rights of association: The most basic element of any sponsorship, this means the right for the sponsor to promote an association between its corporation and/or brand(s), as agreed with the rights-holder, in the public domain and specifically to the key target audiences it hopes to impact through that association.

ROI (Return on Investment): Expressed as a percentage, this is a financial measurement of the efficiency of an investment. It is calculated based on the number of times the net benefits (benefits minus costs) exceed (or are less than) the original investment.

ROO (Return on Objectives): This is a non-financial measure, often expressed by a traffic light system, which presents current performance of a sponsorship in achieving the main objectives of the sponsorship by the investor.

Sponsor: A person, brand or corporation that gives money to a project, individual, etc., for a specific commercially orientated purpose, in exchange for directly related benefits such as publicity, hospitality or sales opportunities.

Sponsorship package: The specific combination of rights/benefits made available through contract to a sponsor by a rights-holder.

Sponsorship tracker: A regular survey carried out by a brand to ascertain the impact of a sponsorship on perceptions and reported usage of that brand.

Tangible assets: Elements of a sponsorship that can be given a specific value either directly (e.g. the cost of a hospitality ticket) or indirectly (e.g. the value of the time a brand is exposed on screen during broadcast coverage, based on the cost of buying equivalent advertising).

Term: The contractual length of a sponsorship relationship between a company and a rights-holder, usually expressed in months or years.

Title Sponsor: The most senior sponsor a property can acquire where the sponsor's name is integrated with the property's name.

Valuation: The process of calculating the value of a sponsorship, based on quantifying the cost of the various tangible elements and deriving a value for intangible elements.

Value in Kind (VIK): Where sponsors provide goods and services to the sponsored property in full or part payment for their rights of association. These goods and services may be budget-relieving (e.g. provision of timing services by a watch brand to an athletics meeting) or may enhance the target audiences' experience of a sponsored activity (e.g. provision of mobile phone recharging points at a music festival).

White Knight: A 'friendly investor' who provides financial and/or other support to a rights-holder free or at a more favourable cost than normal market rates in return for personal satisfaction, recognition or status enhancement by association e.g. individuals who own football clubs where they choose to invest their personal money in purchasing better players than the normal operating performance of the club would be able to support.

INDEX

Compiled by Indexing Specialists (UK) Ltd